A
LANGUAGE
of
REVERENCE

A LANGUAGE *of* REVERENCE

William Sinkford · David Bumbaugh
Laurel Hallman · Sharon Welch
Thandeka

Edited by
DEAN GRODZINS

Meadville Lombard Press
Chicago, Illinois

A Language of Reverence
Ed. by Dean Grodzins
Copyright © 2004 by Meadville Lombard Theological School

First Edition 2004

Meadville Lombard Press
5701 S. Woodlawn Avenue
Chicago, IL 60637

Cover design, cover art, book design, and typesetting by Dan Doolin

"First Lesson," from *Letter from a Distant Land* by Phillip Booth, copyright © 1957 by Phillip Booth. Used by permission of Viking Penguin, a division of Penguin Group (USA) Inc.

"The Rowing Endeth," from *The Awful Rowing Toward God* by Anne Sexton. Copyright © 1975 by Loring Conant, Jr., Executor of the Estate of Anne Sexton. Reprinted by permission of Houghton Mifflin Company. All rights reserved.

"Return to Laughter" from *The Religious* by Sharon Welch. Copyright © 2002 by Blackwell Publishing, Oxford, England. Used with permission from the publisher.

ISBN: 0-9702479-7-4

Printed in the United States of America

Contents

PREFACE

~~~~~~~~~~~~~~~~~~~~~~~~~~~~~

Dean Grodzins

Unitarian Universalists are talking a lot right now about the "language of reverence." The topic became hot in January 2003, when a Fort Worth, Texas, newspaper reported that William G. Sinkford, the president of the Unitarian Universalist Association, had preached a sermon to the First Jefferson Unitarian Universalist Church calling for UUs to add the word *God* to the UUA statement of Principles and Purposes. Sinkford promptly issued a statement declaring that he had been misinterpreted. Although in his sermon, "The Language of Faith," he had expressed "wonderment" that the Principles and Purposes lacked "traditionally religious" language, he had not called for their revision, but more broadly for UUs to reclaim a "vocabulary of reverence," including the word *God*. The newspaper issued a clarification. Soon, every UU with access to the World Wide Web seemed to know about the Fort Worth incident, and most had an opinion about it. Sinkford took advantage of this attention, during subsequent months, to press his point. He urged UUs to reflect more deeply on how they speak about their religion.[1]

They responded. Scores of UU ministers preached about the "language of reverence," dozens of letters on the subject were written to the *UU World*, and hundreds of e-mails were sent to a special "communications forum" at the UUA website. The "language of reverence" became a major issue at the 2003 UU General Assembly, in Boston, and promises to be a major one again at the 2004 GA in Long Beach. The discussion about "reverence" was loud enough that even non-UUs noticed it. The *New York Times*, the *Washington Post*, the *Los Angeles Times*, and the *Boston Globe*, among other newspapers, published articles about the UU debate. I have found a sermon referring to Bill Sinkford's statements preached by a leading Seventh Day Adventist educator.[2]

For UUs, the discussion, although wide-ranging, has revolved more or less around two big questions: "Are we talking about religion in a way adequate to our needs as a religious community?" and "What are we talking about when we talk about religion?" The six pieces in this collection address these questions in different ways.

In President Sinkford's now famous Fort Worth sermon, "The Language of Faith," he conceives of his personal religious journey as one from a youthful, ardent atheism to a more mature theism. Although he insists, "'Religious language' doesn't have to mean 'God talk,'" he challenges UUs to be "secure enough, [and] mature enough" to appreciate a language "that would allow us to capture the possibility of reverence, to name the holy, to talk about human agency in theological terms."

In the sermon, Sinkford acknowledges his debt to an address written in 2001, "Towards a Humanist Vocabulary of Reverence," by David E. Bumbaugh, a noted UU minister, educator, and Humanist.[3] Bumbaugh observes that Humanists have "lost the vocabulary of reverence," which they must reclaim if they are again to set the agenda for religious discourse in the broader culture. He then shows what a humanist vocabulary of reverence might look like, eloquently and passionately employing the lexicon of science.

At the 2003 GA, Bumbaugh returned to the topic of his earlier address with a lecture entitled "Is there a Humanist Vocabulary of Reverence?" Bumbaugh here argues that in our ironically "postsecular" era, traditional religious language "has been so corrupted and exploited as to fail to convey the very depths of reverence the times call for."

Another notable talk delivered at the 2003 GA was the annual Berry Street Essay, "Images for Our Lives," by Laurel Hallman, one of the most prominent UU ministers. Hallman argues for the deep importance of poetry to ministry and to devotional practice. Poetry, she believes, provides a language that "opens up rather than shutting off," that "points beyond rather than positing definitions," that "connects us with the yearning of all humankind, rather than setting us apart as literal in our rejection." Religious language need not be traditional, she believes, but it does need to be metaphorical, and so able to indicate "something much deeper than it could name."

In Sharon Welch's provocative, challenging piece, "Return to Laughter,"[4] this UU theological ethicist cautions us about "the power and peril of the religious and of all religious discourse." Writing as someone who "does not desire God," and who is suspicious of religious discourse, she approaches the problem of religious language with the understanding that religion is amoral. Any attempt to distinguish between false and true religion is only a "dualistic game," because "the language of freedom and openness to others, the language of love and justice, coheres with ecstasy and claim of the religious as easily, but *no more easily*, than the language of exclusion and self righteousness." The moral purposes of religion may be achieved through an "a-theology" of wonder, suffering, memory, and desire, although never achieved with certainty. She concludes by renouncing all self-righteous religious language—traditional, modern, or post-modern—and calling instead for "generous laughter." Such laughter "relishes the irony of knowing that that which funds our morality is itself amoral, and morality, far from being the demand or gift of the divine, is the perilous and at times beautiful human response to the energy and wonder of life."

The final essay in the collection is "New Words for Life," by Thandeka, a systematic theologian and UU minister. She calls attention to a foundational problem for religious liberals: What is human nature? She points out that UUs affirm two conflicting doctrines of human nature—a conflict she illustrates with a perceptive study of a historical dispute between William Ellery Channing and Hosea Ballou. Thandeka argues that without a coherent doctrine of human nature, UUs cannot talk consistently about a common faith tradition. She employs a new approach to the problem, which she calls Affect Theology. It employs contemporary research from the neurosciences as well as studies of historical theology, particularly the work of Friedrich Schleiermacher, to demonstrate that all religious experience has a "common biological foundation" in affective change. On the basis of this insight, Thandeka not only can make new use of traditional religious language, but she can also resolve the UU conflict over human nature. In this way, Thandeka, who first proposed to me the idea for this anthology, provides the book with a hopeful conclusion. She indicates how UUs may celebrate their diverse theological claims while affirming that which they have in common.

These six essays may be seen as the continuation of a long, fruitful conversation on religious language in the Unitarian, Universalist, and UU traditions. The Transcendentalists and the authors of the first Humanist Manifesto, for example, each introduced important new ways of understanding religious language and religion itself. May the current discussion about reverence do the same.

Meadville Lombard Theological School
Chicago, Illinois
28 April 2004

NOTES

---

[1] Jim Jones, "Unitarian Universalists may add 'God' to their beliefs," *Fort Worth Star-Telegram* (January 13, 2003); "Clarification," *Fort Worth Star-Telegram* (January 23, 2003); William Sinkford, "A Statement from President William G. Sinkford" [e-mail to the Unitarian Universalist Minister's Association Chat], January 15, 2003; Sinkford, "Share the Good News with a world that badly needs it," *Unitarian Universalist World* 17:2 (March/April 2003), p. 9; Sinkford, "Language of Reverence: A Response [to Rebecca Parker]," *Journal of Starr King School for the Ministry* [on-line] (Spring 2003), <http://www.sksm.edu/info/journal_images/sinkford.pdf>; Sinkford, "In from the margins," *Religious Humanism* 37 (2003), pp. 44–52.

[2] Letters, *Unitarian Universalist World* 17:4 (July/August 2003); "Reclaiming a Vocabulary of Reverence within Unitarian Universalism," Communications Forum, <www.uua.org/programs/discussion/language/index.html> (viewed April 26, 2004); Richard Higgins, "A heated debate flares in Unitarian Universalism," *New York Times* (May 17, 2003), p. B6; Kevin Eckstrom [Religious News Service], "Request for reverent talk inflames debate," *Washington Post* (May 24, 2003), p. B9; Eckstrom [Religious News Service], "Unitarians debate how to talk about God," *Los Angeles Times* (May 24, 2004), p. B32; Michael Paulson, "Words of 'reverence' roil a church: In Boston, Unitarian Universalists ponder the nature of their faith," Boston Globe (June 28, 2003), p. A1; "Unitarians' Big Forum a Time for Questioning," *Los Angeles Times* (July 12, 2003), p. B23; Gordon Bietz, Reverence, Georgia Cumberland Camp Meeting Sunday School, Collegedale, Tenn., May 30, 2003 <http://president.southern.edu/sermons/reverence.rtf> (viewed April 26, 2004).

[3] Originally published (in a form slightly different from the one here), in *Religious Humanism* 35:1 & 2 (Winter/Spring 2001), pp. 49–59.

[4] Originally published in *The Religious*, ed. John D. Caputo (Malden, Mass., Oxford: Blackwell, 2002), pp. 301–317.

THE
LANGUAGE OF FAITH

William G. Sinkford

First Jefferson Unitarian Universalist Church
January 12, 2003

L et me first bring you greetings from the larger family of
faith of which this congregation is a part. The Unitarian
Universalist Association is nothing more than the coming
together of now 1,050 free liberal religious congregations like
this one. And I'm very pleased to tell you the state of the association today is strong and vibrant. Unitarian Universalism has
grown in numbers in each of the last twenty years, but far more
important than that growth in numbers is a growing ability for
Unitarian Universalism to claim its good news and to live out a
ministry that can help to heal our hurting world in these troubled
and troubling times.

I believe that Unitarian Universalism is growing up. It's
growing out of a cranky and contentious adolescence into a more
confident maturity in which we can not only claim our Good
News, the value we have found in this free faith, but also begin to
offer that Good News to the world outside these beautiful sanctu-
ary walls. There is a new willingness on our part to come in from
the margins.

I spent some time in early November in Dallas with the
President's Council, a group of staunch UUA supporters who serve
as advisors to the Association. The keynote presentation was given

1

by Marlin Lavenhar, the dynamic young senior minister serving at All Souls, Tulsa. In his talk, Marlin wrestled with finding a way to describe and talk about Unitarian Universalism. He told us about a painting he had commissioned to describe our faith, a painting that now hangs in the vestibule of All Souls. The painting depicts a colonial table, representing the roots of Unitarian Universalism in this country. And there are some books on the table: the Bible, recognizing the Judeo-Christian origins of this faith; a volume of Emerson, who taught that individual experience is a key source of religious faith and life; and one unnamed volume indicating that, for us, revelation is not sealed. There's a spray of flowers representing the diversity of persons who call themselves Unitarian Universalist and the diversity of spiritual paths we follow. Marlin is clearly trying to find another way to talk about our faith, and this works for him.

The next morning, Jim Sherbloom led the worship—he's a successful business person who is now, in midlife, a divinity student. He tackled the same subject from a liberal Christian perspective. The interesting thing was that neither speaker drew heavily on our Principles and Purposes, which is where most of us turn when we are asked to describe Unitarian Universalism. So I went and reread the Principles and Purposes. I know, I know . . . I'm supposed to know them by heart. But as I reread them, I realized that we have in our Principles an affirmation of our faith that uses *not one single piece of religious language.* Not even one word that would be considered traditionally religious. And that is a wonderment to me; I wonder whether this kind of language can adequately capture who we are and what we're about.

Our Principles and Purposes date to the merger of the Unitarian and Universalist movements in 1961, when the effort to find wording acceptable to all—Unitarian, Universalist, Humanist, and Theist—nearly derailed the whole process.

The current revision of our Principles and Purposes dates back to 1984. It deals with the thorny question of whether or not to mention God or the Judeo-Christian tradition by leaving them out of the Principles entirely, but including them in the section on the *sources* from which our living tradition draws. It was here that we placed reference to "Jewish and Christian teachings, which call us to respond to God's love by loving our neighbors as ourselves," as well as "Humanist teachings, which counsel us to heed the guidance of reason and the results of science, and warn against idolatries of the mind and spirit." And even that compromise went too far for those in our movement who feared "creeping creedalism," and not far enough for those who would have preferred more explicitly religious language.

Given the differences of opinion that needed to be bridged in one document, it's really not surprising that the wording adopted completely avoided anything that smacked of traditional religious language. The Principles and Purposes have become an integral part of our denominational life. Many of our congregations print them on their orders of service. They open our hymnal. They hang in our vestibules. Many of us carry them in our wallets.

They serve us well as a covenant, holding out a vision of a more just world to which we all aspire despite our differences, and articulating our promise to walk together toward making that vision a reality, whatever our theology. They frame a broad ethic, but not a theology. They contain no hint of the holy.

Now while Unitarian Universalists reject any hint of a creed, we do affirm the importance of the individual credo. We are all charged, individually, to pursue our own free and responsible search for truth and meaning. And I wonder whether the language of our Principles and Purposes is sufficient for that purpose. Unitarian Universalist Minister Walter Royal Jones, who headed the committee largely responsible for the current wording, wondered aloud how likely it is that many of us would, on our deathbed, ask to have the Principles and Purposes read to us for solace and support. I fear, in words borrowed from former UUA president Gene Pickett, that "they describe a process for approaching the religious depths but they testify to no intimate acquaintance with the depths themselves."

I would like to see us become better acquainted with the depths, both so that we are more grounded in our personal faith, and so that we can effectively communicate that faith—and what we believe it demands of us—to others. For this, I think we need to cultivate what UU minister David Bumbaugh calls a "vocabulary of reverence."

Now David is a Humanist. And he believes that Humanists, who "once offered a serious challenge to liberal religion, now find [themselves] increasingly engaged in a monologue," largely because of a vocabulary inadequate to engage other people of faith. "We have manned the ramparts of reason and are prepared to defend the citadel of the mind," Bumbaugh writes. "But in the process of defending, we have lost . . . the ability to speak of that which is sacred, holy, of ultimate importance to us, the language that would allow us to enter into critical dialogue with the religious community."

Our resistance to religious language gets reflected, I think, in the struggle that so many of us have in trying to find ways to say who we are, to define Unitarian Universalism. I always encourage people to work on their "elevator speech." Imagine you're on the sixth floor and you're going to the lobby and somebody asks you, "What's a Unitarian Universalist?" What do you say? You've got about forty-five seconds. Here's my current answer: "The Unitarian side of our family tree tells us that there is only one God, one Spirit of Life, one Power of Love. The Universalist side tells us that God is a loving God, condemning none of us, and valuing the spark of divinity that is in every human being. So Unitarian Universalism stands for: one God, no one left behind."

As with every elevator speech, mine is a work in process. It says where I am right now; and it doesn't say anything at all about where you are.

Many Unitarian Universalists, I know, are bothered by the use of the word *God*. I understand that. When I came to Unitarian Universalism I was an ardent, some might even say a rabid, Humanist. If you had told me as a teenager that at age fifty-six I would be an ordained minister, using religious language in this pulpit, and have a prayer life that centered on thankfulness and gratefulness to God, I would have laughed out loud. The Humanist tradition was mine for a long time.

4

But we don't have this all permanently figured out at any discrete moment in time. In my case, it was direct experience of something I hadn't counted on—the kind of "direct experience of transcending mystery and wonder," which we also affirm as a source of our faith tradition—that changed my mind. It happened in the midst of a crisis. My son Billy, then fifteen years old, had overdosed on drugs, and it was unclear whether he would live. As I sat with him in the hospital, I found myself praying. First the selfish prayers for forgiveness . . . for the time not made, for the too many trips, for the many things unsaid, and, sadly, for a few things said that should never have passed my lips. But as the night darkened, I finally found the pure prayer. The prayer that asked only that my son would live. And late in the evening, I felt the hands of a loving universe reaching out—the hands of God, the Spirit of Life. The name was unimportant. I knew that those hands would be there to hold me whatever the morning brought. And I knew, though I cannot tell you how, that those hands were holding my son as well. I knew that I did not have to walk that path alone, that there is a love that has never broken faith with us and never will.

My son survived. But the experience stayed with me. That is my experience, and my vocabulary for that experience. "Religious language" doesn't have to mean "God talk." I'm not suggesting that Unitarian Universalism return to traditional Christian language. But I do feel that we need some language that would allow us to capture the possibility of reverence, to name the holy, to talk about human agency in theological terms—the ability of humans to shape and frame our world guided by what we find to be of ultimate importance. David Bumbaugh observes that a vocabulary of reverence is implicit in Humanism, with its emphasis on human study and understanding of the natural world. Listen to the language he uses:

> Humanism . . . gave us a doctrine of incarnation that suggests not that the holy became human in one place at one time to convey a special message to a single chosen people, but that the universe itself is continually incarnating itself in

microbes and maples, in hummingbirds and human beings, constantly inviting us to tease out the revelation contained in stars and atoms and every living thing.

This is religious language, placing us in a larger context, whispering of a larger meaning, and carrying with it implications for how we should live.

"The power which I cannot explain or know or name I call God," UU minister Forrest Church has written. "God is not God's name. God is my name for the mystery that looms within and arches beyond the limits of my being. Life force, spirit of life, ground of being, these too are names for the unnameable which I am now content to call my God."

I urge each of you to work on your elevator speech. Put a name to what calls you, and ask yourself what it is to which you find yourself called. Do it often; you won't always necessarily come up with the same answer. Practice telling it to others. This is an exercise that can only help deepen our faith; and with a firmer grounding in those depths, I believe we will be better able to reach out to others. We have Good News for a world that badly needs it. But we may need to expand our vocabularies if we are to be able to develop our faith fully in our own lives, and if we are to be able to share it with others.

I want to leave you with a bit of a poem that came to me in an e-mail, by Tom Barrett:

If I say the word God, people run away.
They've been frightened—sat on till the spirit cried
　　"uncle."
Now they play hide and seek with somebody they can't
　　name.
They know he's out there looking for them, and they
　　want to be found,
But there is all this stuff in the way.
I can't talk about God and make any sense,

And I can't not talk about God and make any sense.

So we talk about the weather, and we are talking about God.

My growing belief is that, as a religious community and as individuals, we may be secure enough, mature enough to find a language of reverence, a language that can acknowledge the presence of the holy in our lives.

Perhaps we are ready. Perhaps this faith we love is ready to stop calling itself a movement, and call itself a religion.

Religion: to bind up that which has been sundered. To make connections in a world that would isolate us. To engage in the real journey toward wholeness.

Who knows? Perhaps we're ready.

So may it be.

Amen.

Toward a Humanist
Vocabulary of Reverence

David E. Bumbaugh

Chicago Area Unitarian Universalist Council
Unitarian Church of Hinsdale, Illinois
May 12, 2001

A s an observer of and participant in contemporary Unitarian Universalism, I have found myself of late wondering what has happened to the Humanist witness among us. How has it happened that we, who once seemed to set the agenda for religious discourse, now find ourselves increasingly on the defensive, if not engaged in a monologue? I would submit that to some degree at least we are talking to ourselves because we have allowed ourselves to be defined by the opposition. We have dismissed traditional religion as an atavistic aberration. We have given up the hope of a constructive dialogue. We have manned the ramparts of reason and are prepared to defend the citadel of the mind against a renewal of superstition until the very end. But in the process of defending, we have lost the vocabulary of reverence, the ability to speak of that which is sacred, holy, of ultimate importance to us, the language that would allow us to enter once more into critical dialogue with others. If this be so, then the recovery of a vital vocabulary of reverence is a task of great urgency for those of us who cherish the Humanism tradition.

In attempting to recover that vocabulary of reverence, I find myself, a nonscientist, looking to the speculative sciences for a lexicon. The history of science in the twentieth century was the history of a continuously enlarging understanding of the universe, its evolution, its history, and its structure. We have engaged the universe at the very limits of our capacity. We have explored the world of the microcosm and the world of the macrocosm. We have found at both extremes incredible complexity. And in that complexity is a source of awe and reverence that we can offer as a metaphor in the religious dialogue of our time.

Thus, in high-energy subatomic physics we have encountered a reality that can only be fully explicated in the language of mathematics and that, when translated into our common discourse, confounds all our settled conventions. We have discovered a world in which particles emerge from and return to the undifferentiated void, a world in which particles oscillate in time, between past and future; a world in which particles appear to be in constant communication with each other across vast distances and at speeds greater than the speed of light; a world that, incredibly, is changed and altered by the very fact of observing it; a world in which the distinctions between subject and object disappear. We are not sure what all of this means, but it becomes clear that at this fundamental level of reality, there is no distinction to be made between you and me and the tree and the rock. Ultimately, the more we understand of our universe at this level, the more we are driven to reverence before the mystery of the invisible, ineffable reality in which our quotidian existence is rooted.

At the other extreme, the macrocosmic world, we discover a universe that is larger than we can encompass in our imaginations. Over the past century, our estimates of the age and the expanse of the universe have proven over and over again to be far too modest. As our ability to measure and observe has improved, we have found a universe that is many billions of years old. As our tools have enabled us to look further and further back into the history of that universe, we have been able to write the story of its emergence to within a few seconds of the beginning. We cannot say much about those first few seconds, and we cannot say anything at all that is more than speculation about the time before time. But this much seems clear: The universe, beginning from an unimaginably hot and dense singularity, evolved through a series of stages, each of which produced the conditions necessary for the succeeding stage. Our sun, our solar system, our planet, our own beings are all late stages of this evolving universe. Curiously enough, much of our insight into the early history of the universe emerges from and resonates with our insights into the interaction of subatomic particles, which suggests a strongly recursive universe in which patterns repeat and recur over many scales. The more we understand about the macrocosm, the more reason we have to stand in awe and reverence at the process that shaped and structured its evolution and *our* evolution.

Nor has this been a matter of intellectual satisfaction only. The insights of cosmology and theoretical astronomy have served to tie us ever more tightly into the emerging story of the universe itself. Just as the processes of the subatomic world underlie and ground our daily existence, so the history of the emerging universe continues to work itself out in our ongoing lives. We now understand that the heavy elements—iron, carbon, oxygen, and all the others—were not present in the earliest stages of the evolving universe. In fact, all of those heavy elements were created in the incredible heat and unimaginable pressures at the heart of massive stars. As those stars died in gigantic supernova explosions, all of these elements so essential to the creation of our planet and to the emergence of life were scattered as dust across vast reaches of space. Eventually that dust coalesced under the force of gravity, and planets were born. On some of those planets, life emerged. The history of the universe is our history; we are all of us recycled stardust. In the words of Robert Terry Weston, "out of the stars have we come." Our very existence is rooted in the fundamental processes of the universe itself. How can we not stand in awe before the fact of our emergence as a consequence of those same vast processes that created galaxies, suns, stars, and planets?

The work that has been done in biology during the past century has magnified that sense of reverence and awe. Building on Darwin's work in the middle of the nineteenth century, biologists have presented us with a powerful understanding of how we are rooted in fundamental processes. Thus we know that the evolutionary processes that produced the universe, the galaxies, the stars, and planets continued on this earth changing its landmasses, its oceans, its atmosphere, and its climate. Early and recent investigations place the date closer and closer to the formation of the planet itself. In tidal pools, or in clay beds, or in volcanic vents, life emerged; and from that first life, all living things on this planet emerged. All that lives or ever has lived derives from a single source.

That would be cause enough for awe and reverence, but recent studies in the earth sciences hint that the tale may be even more complicated. Scientists such as James Lovelock suggest that life did not simply emerge on earth, but that life is a defining artifact of the earth; that the earth became a self-regulating, living entity—Gaia; that we do not live on earth, but rather we exist as elements in earth's living system. Biologists such as Lynn Margulis have suggested that the evolutionary concept of the descent of humanity from earlier life forms obscures the incredible complexity and interwoven nature of life. Evolution, in her view, is the result of the complex interaction and integration of organisms with their total environment. She argues that we did not descend from earlier forms, but rather that our existence is the result of the cooperative, symbiotic merging of earlier life forms to produce greater and greater complexity. Margulis would have us understand that those earlier life forms, in many if not all cases, continue to exist, within us as well as apart from us.

Margulis reminds us that within every cell in our bodies there are life forms called mitochondria. These tiny but essential entities are the processors that transform chemicals into usable energy for our bodies. Without mitochondria our lives would not be possible. Yet mitochondria exist quite independently within our cells. They have their own DNA, their own reproductive processes, and their own life cycles. Margulis speculates that early in the evolution of life, some primordial bacterium ingested mitochondria. Rather than being digested, however, the mitochondria set up housekeeping within the cell and in a remarkable symbiotic relationship began supplying energy to the host, allowing for new forms and possibilities to emerge. In these ways, earlier life forms were not overcome, defeated, outgrown, or cast off as new forms emerged. Instead the evidence suggests that at least in some cases, the earlier forms are incorporated in and an integral part of the life of more complex forms. Margulis reminds us that the bacterium from which life emerged was here before we were, continues to be here with us now, and undoubtedly will be here after we have been replaced by some new emergent life.

In recent days and weeks, we have been reminded of our rootedness in the natural processes of life by reports of the results of the human genome project. The mapping of the human genome has reminded us again how clearly we are part of the Gaian system of life. We share more than 90 percent of our genes with other primates; our genome structure is not markedly different from that of fruit flies or mustard plants. We are intimately related to every living thing that creeps, crawls, or flies; to every living thing that is rooted in the earth and reaches for the sun; to every living thing that inhabits the dark depths of the oceans. We are but one form life has taken, one expression of Gaia's living process. One speculates that if the universe is truly as recursive as it seems, perhaps we are to Gaia as the mitochondria are to us.

In a curious way, we carry with us in our bodies the very environment in which we evolved. The heat of our bodies is the heat of stars, tempered to the uses of life. The salt in our blood and in our tears is the salt of ancient oceans, encapsulated and carried with us, generation upon generation, into strange and distant places and circumstances. The past is not dead. It lives in us. The evolutionary universe, the ancient environment, the emergence of complex life—all this is recapitulated in every moment of our existence.

When the original Humanist Manifesto declared that we are part of nature and we have emerged as the result of a continuous process, it not only denied the creation stories of the Western religious traditions, but it also gave us an immensely richer, longer, more complex history rooted in a system that invites not blind faith but challenge and correction and amendment, one that embraces "truth, known or to be known." It also gave us a language of reverence because it provides us a story rooted not in the history of a single tribe or a particular people, but in the sum of our knowledge of the universe itself. It gave us a doctrine of incarnation that suggests not that the holy became human in one place at one time to convey a special message to a single chosen people, but that the universe itself is continually incarnating itself in microbes and maples, in hummingbirds and human beings, constantly inviting us to tease out the revelation contained in stars and atoms and every living thing. A language of reverence for Humanists begins with our understanding of this story as a religious story—a vision of reality that contains the sources of a moral, ethical, transcendent self-understanding.

It is a religious story in that it calls us out of our little local universes and invites us to see ourselves in terms of the largest self we can imagine—a self that was present, in some sense, in the singularity that produced the emergent universe; a self that was present, in some sense, at the birth of the stars; a self that, in some sense, is related through time to every living thing on this planet; a self that contains within it the seeds of a future we cannot imagine in our wildest flights of fancy.

It is a religious story in that it whispers of a larger meaning to our existence, a suggestion that in us the universe is grasping for self-knowledge, for self-understanding, for insight. How we participate in this process, or what the ultimate consequence of this process may be, we cannot know. But if, as the Humanist Manifesto suggests, we are not separate from nature and we are a result of nature's inherent processes, then our struggles with meaning and purpose and our endless search for insight and understanding are not limited in their significance or consequence to the human enterprise alone. Instead they are part of the emergence of the universe itself.

It is a religious story in that it implies a broader ethic for our lives. To understand the human race as related in the most intimate of ways to all living things on this planet; to understand the earth not as the platform on which life exists, but as itself a living being, regulating its complex systems in such a way as to sustain ongoing life; to understand our own physical beings as a congeries of ancient living forms, quietly and unobtrusively contributing to our ongoing existence while pursuing their own mysterious imperatives; to understand ourselves as the incarnation of those same forces and substances and circumstances that produced galaxies and stars and planets is to enlarge our sense of responsibility and our definition of moral living. In light of this enlarged revelation, the ethic of the main chance, the ethic of short-term benefit, the ethic of immediate gratification, and the ethic of tribal values and ethnic identities so prevalent in our world are challenged in the most profound way and found in every case to be inadequate.

We are challenged to recognize the paradox that our individual well-being is rooted in the understanding that at heart we are one with all things and our sense of separateness is an illusion, while at the same time affirming that our individual separateness is a consequence of the drive of the universe for differentiation and complexity. We are driven by our story to seek an ethic that respects the individual and the ground out of which the individual emerges. This implies a deep concern for ecojustice that reaches across class, racial, ethnic, and even species distinctions and embraces a vision that responds to the largest sense of self we are capable of entertaining.

Brian Schwimm has suggested that the religious story for our time is the "universe story." I would add that the human story and the universe story are the same tale. If the Manifesto was right when it insisted that we are part of nature, not separate from it, that we represent a continuing natural process, then it becomes clear that the challenges, the hopes, the dreams, and the aspirations that find expression in our lives are not separate from the context in which we have evolved, in which we are rooted. We are not encapsulated, separated, isolated beings. Whatever we are, the universe is. The reality inside of us and the reality outside of us are ultimately one reality. In us the universe dreams its dreams. In us the universe struggles for a moral vision. In us the universe hopes for new possibilities. In us the universe seeks self-understanding. In us the universe seeks the meaning of existence. I do not mean to suggest that the universe is limited to our expression of it, or that this is the only place where this kind of complexity has arisen. Nor would I suggest that humanity is the only avenue on this planet by which the universe gropes toward self-awareness. I simply argue that our existence, our struggles, and our failures are lent moral significance by the fact that they occur within in a larger context— the largest context our imaginations can conceive—a context grounded in a unified view of existence.

This is a religious story. It invites us to awe. It demands a vocabulary of reverence. It is a story that is uniquely appropriate to the Humanist tradition. It emerges from the scientific enterprise. It seeks to overcome the ancient dualisms that, over the ages, have diminished the human spirit. It offers a clear alternative to the limited faiths and narrow fundamentalisms that compete for the allegiance of the human community—an alternative that does not have to deny the categories and assumptions upon which our daily lives are built, but can embrace the emergent insights and understandings that enlarge our vision of ourselves and the context in which our lives are lived.

Is There a Humanist Vocabulary of Reverence?

David E. Bumbaugh

Unitarian Universalist General Assembly
Boston, Massachusetts
June 30, 2003

I often tell my students that a sermon is not finished when the last word has been down put on paper. Neither is it completed when the last sentence has been spoken. Indeed, the sermon is not complete until the listeners decide what to do with it. Ultimately, the significance of any sermon rests in the minds of the congregation, and over time—often over a long period of time—they will work with the sermon and complete it. Only then, if ever, will the preacher know what that sermon was really about.

I have had occasion these past few months to understand that central truth in a very personal way. Some time ago I delivered an address entitled "Toward a Humanist Vocabulary of Reverence." It was politely received, reprinted in *Religious Humanism*, and represented at the Fourth Annual Boulder International Humanist Institute. It then seemed to disappear from consciousness. I thought that particular effort had been completed.

Imagine my surprise when I opened the pages of the *Unitarian Universalist World* to find sentences from that address quoted by Bill Sinkford in support of his argument for a reengagement with traditional religious language and concepts. Clearly, the meaning of that original address was still being formulated; I am not certain yet just what it all means. Words spoken cannot be unspoken, and once they are spoken, there is no way to control what they will mean to others. Nonetheless, since I am at heart a preacher, I am drawn to visit the topic again, in an effort to discover where I stand now that what I originally said has been amplified and refocused.

Let me be clear at the outset that I believe that Bill Sinkford is asking the right questions and pointing to significant challenges. For much too long, Unitarian Universalists have been busy talking to ourselves and engaging the larger universe of religion with disdain or misunderstanding. Because the world is too dangerous a place to be left to the hands of fanatics—either religious or secular—we have an obligation to engage the conversation and to offer our truths in the marketplace of ideas and values. The time has come for us to refocus our attention from this persistent inward effort to make of this movement an Eden of purity and correctness and toward an engagement in the messy, ambiguous world of conflicting values and competing ideas. Bill is right when he suggests that to begin that engagement, we must have a language of reverence; that is, we must have the ability to speak with power about what is deepest and dearest, about the focus of our ultimate commitment, about the source of human good, about what is so precious to us that we cannot betray it without losing our own souls.

But let me be equally clear that I believe Bill is wrong when he seeks to find that language of reverence in the classical forms and categories of the monotheistic Jewish and Christian traditions. If our facile optimism about the world has been challenged and outdated by the events of our time, so have the traditional language and affirmations been challenged and outdated. Returning to that language and to those categories will not make us relevant; it will make us partners in a conversation about a world that is gone.

One of the realities we have to recognize is that a substantial change has come over our culture during the past decade or so. We used to think that we lived in a secular world in which religion functioned at the margins. Religious thinkers wrote books protesting the exclusion of religion from the vital social conversation of our time—books such as *The Empty Public Square* and *Habits of the Heart.* And because we affirmed the secular as a realm in which the sacred might be encountered, we allowed ourselves to believe that we were the wave of the future.

Well, tides ebb and flow, and waves crash in and recede. Almost without our noticing, something has happened to our secular culture. It has been caught in an ebbing tide. If we look around us, we might discover that we are living in a postsecular world. Religion is suddenly the hot topic at the center of our public life. In bookstores all across the nation, the titles on religious topics have suddenly moved from their ghetto back there in the corner wedged between Philosophy and New Age. They can now be found boldly shelved among fiction and nonfiction in the front of the store.

Now, I know that most of you never watch any television except occasional PBS documentaries and news programs, but should you allow yourself to go slumming through cable channels such as the Discovery Channel, the Learning Channel, Arts and Entertainment, or the History Channel, you might discover that there has suddenly appeared a steady stream of programming concerned with religion. There are documentaries on the discovery of Noah's ark; programs exploring the meaning of the story of Cain's murder of his brother, Abel; programs about the location of Sodom and Gomorra and the Biblical attitudes toward sex; programs about Abraham and Isaac; histories of the emergence of Christianity out of the religious climate at the beginning of the current era; and much more. And these programs are all attracting advertisers who believe that this kind of religious programming will enable them to sell us more deodorant, SUVs, breakfast cereal, and so on.

Nor is television the only place where this shift has occurred. If you listen with a critical ear to the political language of our time, you may discover that a shift away from the secular has occurred there as well. Those of us of a certain age may remember Franklin Roosevelt's speech to Congress on the day after the attack on Pearl

Harbor. It was a passionate, angry, vital speech calling the nation to total war. But its context was political and secular. Roosevelt spoke as a political leader. Contrast that with the reaction of recent presidents to the *Challenger* disaster, to the attack on the Word Trade Center, or to the more recent shuttle disaster. These events did not evoke political or secular language. Rather, we witnessed the president functioning as *pontifex maximus*, the high priest of the nation. Consider any recent State of the Union address. Recent presidents have taken the metaphor of the bully pulpit seriously. Speeches by our national leaders—short on specifics and long on a call to virtue and values—sound more and more sermonic.

In these, and in other ways, we have moved into a postsecular age, an age in which religious language and modes have become the common currency of our public life. If we are going to be part of the conversation, we need to understand the significance of that shift and what it means for those of us who seek to influence the future in creative and life-affirming ways. Politicians and advertisers are far too pragmatic to adopt religious language and themes unless, in so doing, they can engage and exploit some deep and productive cultural currents.

One scarcely noticed consequence of this shift from the secular to the postsecular, however, is a steady trivialization of once powerful traditional religious language. As traditional religious stories are enlisted to sell soap and cereal and automobiles, faith is quietly transformed into a kind of religion-in-general. As the sacred stories begin to be ranged alongside melodramas about visiting angels and extraterrestrials, ghost stories, urban legends, and miraculous escapes from natural catastrophe, *all* are seen as witnessing to the "something more" quality of life. Religion has become part of the entertainment industry; it is used to excite and move and titillate and motivate, but it has been stripped of its power to stand in critical opposition to unexamined but widely shared practices and unconscious but commonly held assumptions.

And as God and the sacred texts are drafted to support political agendas of questionable merit, the very language of faith is emptied of meaning. Empty words begin to evoke a Pavlovian response from the public at large—an invitation not to conversation but to salivation. The once powerful images and metaphors that enabled the religious community to stand in judgment on the powers and principalities of the day are now servants of the status quo, of conventional thinking and practice.

If there is any truth in this evaluation, then to call for us to use traditional language and symbols and concepts to speak about what is deepest and dearest, about what is the focus of our ultimate commitment, about what is the source of human good, about what is so precious to us that we cannot betray it without losing our own souls in the process is to ask us to employ a tongue that has been so corrupted and exploited as to fail to convey the very depths of reverence the times call for.

How, then, can we speak with power to this generation, which continues to flee a sterile secularism in search of deeper meaning, this generation that pleads for bread and is given stones? To attempt to regenerate the old language seems beyond our capacity at this moment. Worse, the attempt seems likely to prove to be another distraction. Clearly we need to engage a different language of reverence.

I believe we have such a language of reverence in our tradition, one that will allow us to speak with power and clarity in the larger religious community. It is a language that has the potential of unshackling the religious vision from its enslavement to the politics and economics of conventional society. The vision I'm talking about has roots in the Transcendentalism of Emerson and Parker and Thoreau; it also has roots in the naturalistic mysticism of Kenneth L. Patton and the theology of Henry Nelson Wieman. Most importantly for our time, it is rooted in the vision of reality and of humanity's place in the world that is emerging from the natural sciences—theoretical physics, astronomy, biology, and chaos theory. It is our language; it is a humanist language of reverence.

The Humanist Manifesto was an invitation to reenvision the religious enterprise and to challenge the prevailing attitudes and assumptions of the religious community. We are now called to renew that undertaking—to find or build a vocabulary of reverence adequate to the vision that is emerging around us. It is a vision that comes as the result of the drive by the universe to know and understand itself. We need a vocabulary adequate to describe a universe that regularly confounds our expectations even as it rewards our attempts to know, by revealing levels of meaning that make contemporary faddish talk of angels and gods and spirits seem trivial and irrelevant. We are children of—expressions of—a universe that is not only "stranger than we know, but stranger than we can know." It is incumbent upon us to challenge the parochial and limited claims of traditional religions with the enlarging, enriching, and reverent story that is our story and their story: the Universe Story.

This religious story needs to be in conversation with other religious traditions, but that conversation cannot take place if we allow our vision to be poured into the old wineskins of impotent categories: the language used to sell cars and toothpaste and morally bankrupt political and economic agendas; the language manipulated to generate a sense of warm comfort in a world growing steadily more dangerous; the language that disguises and eviscerates the radical alternative it offers. We must offer a powerful religious vision conveyed in a language of reverence appropriate to the faith it represents in the marketplace of ideas. If we are able to do that, perhaps we can provoke a real conversation.

IMAGES FOR OUR LIVES

Laurel Hallman

The 2003 Berry Street Essay
Boston, Massachusetts
June 26, 2003

I want to dedicate this essay to the memory of two men who died the same week in March. The first is Harry Scholefield, who was my mentor and friend and partner in the work of articulating a spiritual practice for religious liberals. The second, perhaps unknown to many of you, is Hardy Sanders. A layperson in my congregation in Dallas, Hardy was one of the most passionate, devoted, and generous UUs I have ever known. These two losses, in the midst of all that we have had to bear this year, weighed heavily on me as I prepared this essay.

Each one was devoted to our faith. Yet Hardy felt that we were frittering away our message with petty diversions. And Harry felt that we, especially the UU ministers, were using poems and wisdom literature without having lived them. In many ways their lives and concerns shape what I have to say today.

I want to talk about imagination, specifically *religious* imagination. I want to say that we are in a crisis of language because we have forgotten what religious imagination is and does. The purpose of my essay today is to remind us of the importance of religious imagination in all our varied ministries.

But first let me go back to 1971.

23

I was twenty-eight years old. I was at home with my then one-year-old toddler. Roy Phillips, the new minister at Unity Church-Unitarian in St. Paul, Minnesota, where I was a member, asked me to join a committee he was forming to rewrite the Sunday school curriculum. He was gathering a group of members, mostly teachers, to talk about what was needed. Mary Anderson, who is here today as my guest, was a member of that group of seven. She is Lebanese, was raised a Muslim, and is a devoted UU. She helped us broaden our perspective significantly in those days, which now seem so long ago. Roy said that some members of the congregation had expressed the need for a religious education that centered on traditional religious themes—an education that would help the children to know themselves as religious people. He wanted me to help.

Needing a project with some challenge in those days, I said yes. That project is to a large degree why I stand before you today.

You can ask people what they believe, and they may tell you something halfway interesting. But if you ask them what should be taught to their children, you quickly get down to basics. We were fulfilling the gritty and difficult duty of deciding what to teach our children, and how and why.

The curriculum was called *Images for Our Lives.*

That work, which took up four years of our lives, happened long ago and far away. But I learned two important points that apply to what I want to say today. The first was our decision always to look for the "religious existential dimension" of the story we were teaching, whether the story was from the Judeo-Christian tradition (as we called it in those days), or from our own Unitarian Universalist tradition, or from other world religions. (We gave each of those categories twelve weeks a year.)

We actually devised a chart. It was called "Three Ways of Interpreting a Story." The first section was the "Literal, Popular, Fundamentalist Interpretation." The second section was the "Rational, Critical, Historical Interpretation." And the third was the "Religious, Existential, Spiritual Interpretation."

I was familiar with the first one. I had been raised a fundamentalist. I knew my Bible and the literal interpretation of the stories.

And to some degree, we were familiar with rational, critical, historical interpretations. Although Roy recounted that the Unitarian Sunday school of his youth, in an *attempt* at a rational interpretation, had taught that Jesus had not walked on water, but rather on sandbars.

We had some sense of the new thought that had brought about biblical criticism, and it had more substance than sandbars, we knew. So we made a place in our chart for such interpretations.

It was the third category that most interested us, though: "Religious, Existential, Spiritual Interpretation."

I'm not sure where that phrase came from. It wasn't tied to Existentialism per se. Roy says he used the dictionary definition at first: "grounded in existence or the experience of existence." But after much discussion we decided that the religious existential dimension of each story was to be the center of our work. We would try to find the part of each story that would allow the children to "take the story as an image of their own experience of life."

For example, the story of Noah became less a story about a god who wanted to start things over, and more about an incredible image of a tiny boat—built to specifications, but oh-so small in that huge sea—and Noah, who had been so faithful, left for five months with no horizon and no contact. That was something that resonated for us. And if it didn't resonate with our children at the time, at least they would have it as a container for their life experience in the future.

At some point, we reasoned, if our children were in a life situation with no shore in sight, as if forgotten by their mamas and their papas, and even by God, we wanted them to remember Noah. We wanted them to be connected in a deep way to all those others who had felt forgotten until they sent out a dove and it returned with an olive branch. All those others who had to wait so long for hope to return.

That is why we called it *Images for Our Lives*. Every story we presented, whether Noah or Emerson or Kisogatami, was considered in its religious existential dimension. With the recall of an image, our children could associate their life experiences. Which brings me to the second point I learned while working on that curriculum. We called it the *piñata* effect.

At one of our weekly meetings, we were going over a lesson. It was a good lesson, educationally speaking. The author was quite sophisticated in the development of curriculum. She had created an interesting and compelling lesson that centered on a *piñata*. (Who among us hasn't had a *piñata* at some church event or other?)

When we asked her what the religious existential dimension of the *piñata* lesson was, she couldn't name it. It was interesting culturally, the children would have a great time, it might be group building, but it did not point to anything beyond itself. It could not be grounded in the experience of existence, at least not in the imaginative way in which we had been working. It was simply interesting. She agreed to throw the lesson out.

From then on, whenever we created curriculum that strayed from our purpose of nurturing the religious, existential, and spiritual dimension of our material, we simply said "*piñata*," and out it went.

To this day, when I'm writing a sermon, or preparing a lesson, the word *piñata* will rise up in my consciousness. At that point I realize that no matter how eloquent I have been, no matter how clever, the words are not achieving my purpose, which is to speak to the depth of human experience.

Today one of the reasons we are having a crisis of language among ourselves is that we haven't said "*piñata*" enough. It is because we have been charmed, sometimes by the sound of our own voices, sometimes by the brilliance of our own minds, speaking eloquently about this or that, but forgetting the foundation of our work in the world—the religious existential dimension of life and the communication from person to person and generation to generation of a kind of truth that is based on the reality. As Bernard Meland once said, it is a truth based on the reality "that we live more deeply than we think."[1]

If the religious existential reality is "grounded in the experience of existence," and "we live more deeply than we think," then we had better find ways to say that which is deeper than we can speak.

Now I am keenly aware of my audience here today. Most of us are off the scale when it comes to our verbal abilities. After all, didn't the *Wall Street Journal* recently tell us that the young people in our churches have the highest SAT scores in the nation? We who are the leaders of perhaps the most educated group in the country—though we're embarrassed to admit it—so often forget what we know when it comes to religious language. And we forget that it is our job to teach our congregations what we know.

I recently spoke to our adult Sunday school class in Dallas on the topic "Why I Am Not a Theist." They packed the room to hear what I had to say, because of course they thought I was. Why did they think I was a theist? Because I use the word *God*. Because I pray in the midst of the worship service. I was a bit embarrassed to find that I had failed to make the distinction that the use of metaphors and poetry and scripture has to do with religious imagination, and not with one theological category or another. We had a lively and productive discussion that day, as I spoke about how religious language communicates the depths of experience, and isn't always what it seems.

I remember years ago when the Principles and Purposes were being formulated in meetings all across our continent. Peter Fleck, of beloved memory, was on the committee to synthesize those formulations, and he said that he had noticed a curious thing. When he asked individual UUs where they stood theologically, "They would juxtapose two seemingly opposite theological categories together. Like Christian-Humanist or Agnostic-Christian or Rational-Mystic, refusing to align themselves with one distinct theology." Peter was puzzled by this.

I now think it was the beginning of our attempt to extricate ourselves from the hard theological boundaries with which we had closed ourselves off from one another and from our experience of religious imagination and deep reality.

When I arrived at theological school, I found there were other languages of currency, other ways we were extricating ourselves from the boundaries of theological language and categories. These languages were mainly psychological and political: the psychological to give meaning and the political to give purpose. We learned the language of ethical discourse and the languages of various theologies. But the real categories of discussion among us were psychological and political. Gone were the earlier days of humanist/theist debates. In their place were struggles to integrate our ministries with the problems of the world and the pathologies of our lives.

I was later intrigued by Harry Scholefield's story of having undergone several years of Freudian analysis in Philadelphia. He had been invited into the Psychoanalytic Institute as part of a special program for professionals in areas other than psychology. He ended up immersing himself in analysis. He told the story of the importance of his analysis to his ministry in a Berry Street essay in 1962. He spoke then on the topic "Motivation in the Ministry." His essay was published as "Psychoanalysis and the Parish Ministry: Some Reflections on Unconscious Motivation in Preaching and Present Trends in Pastoral Counseling." Harry could also speak the language of the political life of his times. He was a well-known peace and fair housing activist in San Francisco, where he was minister for most of his career.

During my theological years and afterward, I came to respect deeply the power of psychological and political thought, action, and language in shaping who we are and what we are to do in the world.

I also came to understand that pathology could not be the only focus for our inner work; I saw too many political activists who burned out because their activism was not grounded. There was something else that was needed to deepen our meaning and purpose. That something else was the language of religious imagination.

The problem with language is that those words, those simple individual words are slippery little devils. They don't stay put. I remember my shock, as a junior high student, when I used the word *queer* thinking it meant "odd" and discovering to my dismay that it was a pejorative label for a homosexual.

I was horrified partly because I was in junior high and partly because I hadn't meant what people thought I meant. But I was most horrified that the word didn't mean what I thought it did. Until that point I had assumed that words meant what they meant—that words stood still. They stood firm against all the vicissitudes of life. But in that moment, my faith in language was shaken. Words could add meaning, they could change meaning, and they could turn on you. I was shocked. (I should also add that at that time in my life I was a religious fundamentalist. It may have been more than my faith in *words* that was shaken that day.)

And then I was to discover that a word, for example *God*, could become the victim of what Whitehead called "Misplaced Concreteness." Over time, words could lose their rich, metaphorical, living depth, and become concrete—rigid and lifeless. The imaginative vitality could ebb away. The word *God* could die.

So if words don't stand still; if they are subject over time to misplaced concreteness; if they don't necessarily represent one theology or another; if they are inadequate even when they serve political and psychological purposes, even when they give us some meaning and purpose; if they need to point to the depths of lived experience (the religious existential dimension of life); if we live more deeply than we can think; if we are currently in a crisis of language (which I believe we are); if we are truly to minister in the fields of human need, what will save us from ourselves?

My answer is poetry.

Now if that answer disappoints you, I ask that you stick with me. Let me quickly explain that by poetry I mean words, phrases, and even whole narrative stories that point beyond themselves to the depth of human experience. I believe that poetry is scripture. I believe that scripture is poetry. I believe that poetry is the way deep truth transmitted from person to person and generation to generation. I believe that when Emily Dickinson said "Tell the truth/but tell it slant" she was speaking of metaphorical truth, the poetic truth that nourishes the heart, and opens the mind, and communicates to the depths. By poetry I mean the products of the religious imagination.

First, let me say that I am keenly aware that there are many products of the imagination that are not centered in words. So if poetry seems an extraordinarily limited focus for all the possibilities of metaphorical truth that can communicate the depth, I will admit that it *is*. But again, I want to remember where I am, and who we are, and what we do week after week after week. I know there are many different ministries represented here, and I hope you'll bear with me if I narrow my scope and talk about words and their uses between and among us, acknowledging that music and art and even the silences of the soul are more profound than I could speak today. But speaking I am, and so we're going for religious imagination, the verbal expression of the depth of human experience.

Second, let me say that by religious imagination, I am not speaking only of the products of the imagination that have explicit religious references.

Consider Philip Booth's wonderful poem "First Lesson," about teaching his daughter to swim:

> *Lie back, daughter, let your head*
> *be tipped back in the cup of my hand.*
> *Gently, and I will hold you. Spread*
> *your arms wide, lie out on the stream*
> *and look high at the gulls. A dead-*
> *man's float is face down. You will dive*
> *and swim soon enough where this tidewater*
> *ebbs to the sea. Daughter, believe*
> *me, when you tire on the long thrash*
> *to your island, lie up, and survive.*
> *As you float now, where I held you*
> *and let go, remember when fear*
> *cramps your heart what I told you:*
> *lie gently and wide to the light-year*
> *stars, lie back, and the sea will hold you.*[2]

This poem has not one traditional religious word in it. And yet it associates to deep realities beyond itself and across generations of human experience.

For a time I thought this would be enough. There are certainly enough images and stories out there to take us to the heights and depths of human experience without having to bother with traditional religious language. These poems and narratives would have to fulfill certain criteria, of course. They would have to take on associative meeting; they would have to break concrete meanings open; they would have to be relational; they would have to name experience in a way that takes us beyond ourselves, and even beyond the experience itself. Surely there is enough spoken and written in the literature of humankind to be able to speak to human experience without having to evoke a God or think about prayer or use any of the words that have specifically religious associative meanings—those meanings that are so encumbered as to be almost impossible to use. Or so it seemed to me at the time.

"First Lesson" should be enough.

But then I heard a simple story about a Russian Orthodox icon. The priest explained that the value of the icon was in its ability to teach the people who sat with it. "They didn't analyze it. It taught them," he said. ("Not very American," he added.) Being from a more plain tradition, I never pursued iconography. I have always worried about idolatry, but that simple explanation changed how I thought about the traditional words of Western religion. I couldn't drop them. They had evoked too much for too many people over too long a time, and I needed to stay connected to the human struggles and the human understandings they represented, if only to inform my own. The word *God* might have become concretized. The word *God* might even have died. But I could not ignore all that it represented before it was rigidified into a state of rigor mortis.

Suzanne Langer, in her book *Philosophy in a New Key,* was also helpful on this point. She says: "This tendency is comprehensible enough if we consider the preeminence with which a named element holds the kaleidoscopic flow of sheer sense and feeling. For as soon as an object is denoted, it can be held, so that anything else that is experienced at the same time, instead of crowding it out, is experienced with it, in contrast or in unison or in some other way.... A word fixes something in experience, and makes it the nucleus of memory, an available conception. Other impressions group themselves round the denoted thing and are associatively recalled when it is named."[3]

Who was I to drop these words that had meant so much to our very own spiritual ancestors, as well as generations of human seekers, even if the associations might be complex? Perhaps the word *God* wasn't as dead as I had thought.

Interestingly, I remembered, too, that Harry Scholefield had called his Freudian analysis "the relentless practice of association." He said that whatever associated to the topic at hand in analysis had to be faced. It was a difficult practice, he said. And one that took years to embrace fully.

Later in his life, Harry was to move his relentless practice of association into his meditative times, waiting for the words of poets and scribes to associate with each other, and with his lived experiences. "Sometimes," he said, "Walt [that would be Walt Whitman] would arrive, and have a comment or two, and then Emily [that would be Emily Dickinson] would join in." He went on, "Sometimes I had a sense of Presence, of being encompassed by something larger than I was in those moments, perhaps through the word of a Psalmist, and we would all have a conversation."

Language is a relational system, Suzanne Langer says. A word, especially one of depth of experience, has many associations, and our job is to be open to those associations. They take us deeper than we can think because we are not observers. We are participating in the conversation with our very lives.

The best example I know of this is by Anne Sexton in "The Rowing Endeth," from *The Awful Rowing Toward God*:

> *I'm mooring my rowboat*
> *at the dock of the island called God.*
> *This dock is made in the shape of a fish*
> *and there are many boats moored*
> *at many different docks.*
> *"It's okay," I say to myself,*

with blisters that broke and healed
and broke and healed—
saving themselves over and over.
And salt sticking to my face and arms like
a glue-skin pocked with grains of tapioca.
I empty myself from my wooden boat
and onto the flesh of The Island.

"On with it!" He says and thus
we squat on the rocks by the sea
and play—can it be true—
a game of poker.
He calls me.
I win because I hold a royal straight flush.
He wins because He holds five aces.
A wild card had been announced
but I had not heard it
being in such a state of awe
when He took out the cards and dealt.
As he plunks down His five aces
and I sit grinning at my royal flush,
He starts to laugh,
the laughter rolling like a hoop out of His mouth
and into mine,
and such laughter that He doubles right over me
laughing a Rejoice-Chorus at our two triumphs.
Then I laugh, the fishy dock laughs
the sea laughs. The Island laughs.
The Absurd laughs.

Dearest dealer,
I with my royal straight flush,
love you so for your wild card,
that untamable, eternal, gut-driven ha-ha
and lucky love.[4]

I didn't play cards when I was a fundamentalist, and for sure God didn't! The God I knew, even with all *His* spoken and unspoken associations, concretized as *He* was, is broken open into a dealer who deals, not the plan for my life, but a wild card, "untamable, eternal, gut-driven *ha-ha* and lucky love."

How could I not welcome such an intrusion into my solidified vision?

If, as Langer asserts, language is a relational system, with associations forming themselves around a more concretized concept, then it is hubris for us to believe that we can cut out some words, and put others on the back burner, for they will find their way back into consciousness, often in surprising ways.

As Harry used to say, "They just put up a hand, saying, "Wait, I have something to say."

What we need to do, then, is to break open these concretized words, to juxtapose them with words that create cognitive dissonance. For it is in the spaces between the juxtapositions that new associations are created.

The first inkling I had of this was when we began to use the pronoun *She* with reference to God. People laughed nervously when they heard this for the first time. People laughed. It was so strange. So odd.

The idea that metaphors that have suffered misplaced concreteness can be brought to life by simply juxtaposing them in surprising ways is almost too simple. It creates a cognitive dissonance in the listener that breaks them open—not to new *definitions* of God, or whatever element of mystery you are attempting to point toward, but to a small portion of reality that they have experienced. Remember, we're talking about the religious existential dimension of life, not rigid definitions. We're talking about the products of the imagination here. We're pointing, not positing.

I want to mention another element of our linguistic crisis: the language of yearning. There's more to it than that, but let's start there.

Early in my ministry I began to question why people were coming to see me. The problems and issues they brought into my study were posed in psychological terms. I knew that there were enough therapists in town to cover the needs of my whole congregation. "Why are they coming to me?" I asked myself. Perhaps, I answered myself, it was because I was a minister. They didn't have the language to speak it, but they had the depth to feel it. They needed *spiritual* counsel.

One day, feeling rather bold, I asked a person who was in my office if she had prayed about her situation. Without hesitation, she said, "Yes. I feel like a child again, but I can't help myself."

It gave me some traction, a place from which to minister. "Shall we pray about it now?" I asked.

She said yes, and we did.

I can't say it was transformative for her, but I had the keen sense that at some level she expected that was what we would do.

I will say that it changed my understanding about why people were coming to me. It was because I was a minister! They expected me to ask them about things like prayer. They expected me to take them somewhere beyond that childhood version of prayer they remembered.

I have learned always to ask.

I remember once visiting a woman who did not have long to live. She was a confirmed skeptic. I knew that. But I thought, perhaps, in this tender moment, she might want her minister to pray her through.

"Would you like me to pray?" I asked.

She was so forceful in her "No" that I actually thought I might have given her a renewed reason to live!

So I want you to know that I'm not advocating one path. These are products of the imagination, not definitions of ministerial methods. With that caveat, I will say that I am convinced that our congregations need a vocabulary of yearning. And that is prayer. They need an opportunity to name their relationship with life in relational words, in poetry, in metaphor. They need to pray.

I was fortunate that when I went to Dallas prayer was already part of the service. Slowly I introduced relational words. Slowly I directed the prayer to "God of many names, and mystery beyond all our naming. . . ." Slowly I began to ask for help and comfort and wisdom and strength. Slowly I began to name individuals who needed our prayer, and with whom we were celebrating. I gave thanks for new babies and grieved over lost loved ones—naming fathers and mothers, and sisters and brothers who had died. I prayed about our inadequacy to face the pain of our days.

This is not a rational posit to a responding deity. It is not a posture of groveling. It is an expression of our yearning, our grief, and our gratitude. It has become an expression of our congregation as a whole.

Every once in a while someone asks me "who" I think I'm praying to. I recall the good advice from twelve-step programs. "Just take care of your side of the street," that sage wisdom goes. And that's what I do with prayer. I take care of my side of the street—with my gratitude, amazement, praise, fear, anger, and hurt—and the side of the street my congregation is on. I figure the other side of the street can take care of itself and we can save the theological discussions for later. It answers the question of "who" by saying the question is not germane to this relational approach to prayer. A relational approach is concerned with articulating yearning from my "side of the street," not defining who is on the other side of the conversation, just as I would not worry about defining "who" I am speaking to, in a relationship with a person. I would simply speak.

I was lucky enough to inherit from Bob Raible's ministry in the Dallas church, the closing to the prayer, which I commend to you. People, including my late friend Hardy Sanders, have said that they wept when they first heard the words:

"We pray in the names of all those, known and unknown, present and absent, remembered and forgotten. We pray in the names of all the helpers of humankind."

This is language that opens up rather than shutting off.

This is language that points beyond rather than positing definitions.

This is language that connects us with the yearning of all humankind, rather than setting us apart as literal in our rejection, closed in our disdain, set apart in our determination to reject language that will not imagine anything beyond what we see and know. Remember, we do live more deeply than we think. We must, as religious leaders, point through our thinking, connecting to the depths of life, where our people live.

I once was taken with the idea put forth by two therapists about the importance of having a "richness of model." They said that when people came with this or that difficulty, they found that their ability to overcome their problem was largely based in their richness of model. If one had a thin model of life and its possibilities, he or she would have little probability of finding new ways of living that would improve existing relationships. If the model of life was varied and open, with many possibilities envisioned, the person would have a much higher probability of adapting to new ways of being.[5]

What might contribute to a person's richness of model? I wouldn't want to limit such a discussion among us, but I am convinced that before education, before life experience, before even the quality of our relationships, a possible contributing factor to a person's richness of model is religious imagination.

For that is where we name our experience; that is where we forge our relationship to what is; that is where we know who we are, what we are living for, and where our yearning is.

For what is the poetic but an attempt to name experience in a relational way? I can hear Walt (that would be Whitman) saying:

You air that serves me with breath to speak!
You objects that call from diffusion and give them shape!
You light that wraps me and all things in delicate
    equable showers!
You paths worn in the irregular hollows by the roadsides!
I believe you are latent with unseen existences, you are
    so dear to me.[6]

Religious imagination opens us to an encompassing "You" of life that takes on a complexity of relationship (a richness of model) we can nurture and cultivate, for ourselves and for those with whom we minister.

But then there is Harry Scholefield raising a hand and saying, "Wait. I have something to say. This isn't about preaching, or counseling, or the various ways we speak in our ministries—it is about our own depth as ministers. It is about living into the language of *our* ministries.

"How's *your* meditative life," he would say to me. "You talk about *Images for Our Lives*. You mean images for *our* lives. Yours and mine. For how can we speak to the depths if we are living in the shallows of busyness, where more than a few of us abide."

Late in Harry's ministry he significantly changed the way he worked, trying to allow his ministry to arise more from the depths of his experience than from the demands of the moment. He had always memorized poetry, and so he increasingly turned to the poetry he had memorized as a kind of mantra for meditation.

He said that the more he leaned into wisdom words from scripture and poets, and even such prose as the Gettysburg Address and Lincoln's Second Inaugural—the more he sat with those words—the more they began to associate with other poems, with experiences in his life, and with creative realities entering into the conversation.

What Langer had said about the associative properties of language suddenly became substantive in a person whose life and practice I could see. Here was a man who might have called himself a Religious Humanist. He certainly wasn't a Christian or a Theist. He worried over the use of the word *God*, and yet he found solace in the 139th Psalm; found grounding for his activism in the words of the Prophets, especially Amos; and found his inner life peopled with Rumi and Rilke.

Here was associative devotional practice.

Juxtaposing images in a sermon, or using the words *God/she* to break open the concretizing tendency of language and refresh meaning, are less tools of the trade, and more sources for the soul, which is certainly where our ministries have to originate if we are to do any good. Memorizing scripture and poetry and prose has become a spiritual practice for me, and a way into the spiritual lives of the very real people with whom I minister.

In other words, juxtaposing words and images began within my own being, out of my own spiritual practice, creating the kind of cognitive dissonances that keep my life open and fresh.

Some of us have found poetry. We certainly have enough inspirational writing to keep us going for the next century. But at the end of the poem with which we begin a board or program council meeting—when we all pause for an appropriately thoughtful moment before plunging into the business at hand—at that moment, where is the "living word"? Where is the word of our lives, of our hearts? Harry was right. It's where we live. And unless our lives are expressed in those words of inspiration, they will go the way of all concretized words, into the hardened blocks of calcified religion, of no living use or help in the pains and joys of our lives.

I don't know about your congregation, but mine has within it the full range of human joy and despair. I learned in my years at a church in a college town that the people didn't come to church to have an adjunct to the university. They came to church to nourish their spiritual natures, to give voice to their hopes and their despair, to speak depth-to-depth with others, finding their natures beyond psychological language, and their purpose beyond political categories. They came to find meaning, purpose, and understanding in the religious language of the centuries, of necessity broken open yet one more time through association, through cognitive dissonance, through the naming of common yearnings and hopes as well as failures.

We not only need to invite poets into the rooms of our hearts, but we need to invite our spiritual ancestors as well. They are raising a hand, wanting to be heard. If we say, "We'll listen, but don't use any words that have become solidified in the meantime, no matter how fulsome they were for you," we will have cut ourselves off, not only from our spiritual DNA, but also from one part of the conversation that we desperately need to have.

Our president has called us to a language of reverence. We *need* a language of reverence. We need a language of forgiveness. We need a language of reconciliation, a language of hope, a language that gives voice to despair. That language has for many centuries, and in countless cultures, been metaphorical. It has pointed beyond itself to something much deeper than it could name. It is our turn to keep such language alive, hold it to our hearts, and speak to the depths of those who so desperately need our good word.

NOTES

[1] Bernard Meland, *Fallible Forms and Symbols: Discourses on Method in a Theology of Culture* (Philadelphia: Fortress Press, 1976), p. 184.

[2] Philip Booth, *Letter from a Distant Land: Poems by Philip Booth* (New York: Viking, 1957), p. 60.

[3] Suzanne K. Langer, *Philosophy in a New Key: A Study in the Symbolism of Reason, Rite and Art* (1941; 3d ed., 1970; Cambridge, Mass.: Harvard University Press, 1976), p. 100.

[4] Anne Sexton, *The Awful Rowing Toward God* (Boston: Houghton Mifflin, 1975), pp. 85–86.

[5] Richard Bandler and John Grinder, *The Structure of Magic: A Book About Language and Therapy* (Palo Alto, Cal.: Language and Behavior Books, 1975). Also referenced in Roy Phillips's essay "Preaching as a Sacramental Event," in William F. Schulz, ed., *Transforming Words: Six Essays on Preaching* (Boston: Skinner House, 1984), p. 25.

[6] Walt Whitman, "Song of the Open Road," in *Leaves of Grass, The "Death Bed" Edition* (New York: Random House, Modern Library Paperback, 2001), p. 185.

RETURN TO LAUGHTER

Sharon Welch

2002

W hat are we doing when we do theology? What types of
claims are we making about "beings-beyond being?"[1]
What "symbolic of desire" is manifest in our con-
cepts and our definitions of religious truth?[2] What realities are we
invoking, what behaviors, what state of mind do we conjure in our
prayers, rituals, and theological and philosophical explorations of
the sacred and the profane?

We often like to think that there was a time when it was easy
to know what we were doing when we spoke of gods or "convened
the ritual cosmos"[3]; we responded to the unambiguous demand of
divine revelation; we witnessed to the transformative power of religious experience; we participated in communal rituals that sustained the world.

While I doubt that religious experience and activity within
fundamentalisms of the present or in premodern religious communities was as simple as it appears to us who live in a postmodern world, we can be certain of one thing; it is not simple now, and
is not simple for us. After deconstruction, each term of our discourse, each gesture of our rituals, each movement of desire is seen
as contested, indeterminate, and socially constructed. Not only are
our concepts, gestures, and desires constructed, and indeterminate,

but they are implicated in master narratives that help sustain oppression, domination, violence, and exclusion.[4]

The work of philosophers of religion and of theologians now highlights these dual concerns. The god of metaphysics and the methods and claims of onto-theology are discredited as much for their legitimization of oppression as for their conceptual idolatry. Where does this leave us theologically? What are our options in the present moment?

In this essay I could take up the deconstructive task as described by Grace Jantzen, a critique and alternative that is a therapeutic intervention in a dangerous symbolic of desire.[5] Placing my work in the camp of feminist theology, I could take up Irigaray's "becoming divine," and with Jantzen construe a symbolic of desire based on natality rather then death.[6] In short, I could propose another symbolic that is more fitting to the epistemic challenges of postmodernity, and more suited to the imperative of establishing justice. In contrast to all of these philosophers, I could argue that each is still implicated in logics of oppression that elide the power of finitude and ambiguity, and provide a more adequate symbolics of natality and finitude, one informed by an African, African-American, and American Indian symbolics of balance and beauty.

I could play the dualistic game of point-counterpoint, but I will not. I will not repeat the cut, the division into legitimate/illegitimate, natality/death, faith/religion for a simple reason. To take refuge in such a divide (or even in the possibility of such a divide) is to miss the power and peril of the religious and of all religious discourse. "In itself" (a loaded phrase to be sure) religious experience is profoundly meaningful, central to a community's and an individual's sense of identity, and, at the same time, intrinsically amoral.

I once claimed that the cause of justice was better served if, rather than focus on God as the source of "right relations" we saw divinity as being "right relations," thus construing divinity as a quality of relations, an adverb rather than a noun.[7] At that time I limited divinity to *right* relations, a move similar to that of other liberal and liberation theologians who describe God as the force of creativity and justice. Now I see creativity and intense relatedness as themselves amoral, and the task of giving them moral expression is socially and culturally mediated, perilous, and haphazard.

In describing what this means for positive, although intrinsically ambiguous appreciation of spirituality, I emphasize an ironic spirituality that holds the paradox of being founded by that which is also amoral, contingent, and malleable.

I speak for those who find the Barthian and Derridean escape untenable: your encounter with the divine is religious and a projection and we have received a revelation which has shattered even the pretensions of our Protestant religion and natural theology (Barth) or, your vision of justice is an idolatrous concrete messianism while ours, in its radical openness, in its "universal longing and restlessness," is free from the projections that create religious violence, coercion, and fanaticism."[8] In much (all?) western philosophies of religion and theology we find an odd logic indeed, so sensitive to the potential and actual harm of other religious symbolics, so certain that we have found the key that can help us escape the same dynamic (the Protestant principle, Derrida's messianic affirmation, which is not a concrete messianism).

Just as there is no *universal* longing for a total surprise, there is no definitive escape from injustice and error. I will describe a symbolic of the "fully now" (not the *tout autre*), a desire for the plentitude of presence that can also evoke justice, freedom, and respect. Yet this form of religious discourse stands *alongside*, not over-against, Marion's construals of God beyond Being and the symbolic of the gift, alongside Jantzen's and Irigaray's "becoming divine," alongside Derrida's *tout autre* and Lévinas's God whose name is the call for justice.[9] Although this construal differs in its placement of error and injustice, (acknowledging the amorality at the core of the religious), *it is not, for that reason, more likely, nor less likely than any other construal to lead to justice or injustice.* Here I draw on Nietzsche's notion of the longest lie—the belief that "outside the haphazard and perilous experiments we perform there lies something (God, Science, Knowledge, Rationality, or Truth) which will, if only we perform the correct rituals, step in to save us."[10]

43

It is important to realize that not one of these variants of religious experience (*ours included*), not one of these construals of the divine or divinities or spiritualities, inevitably and reliably leads to ethical action. The construal of divinity as wholly other, as the excess of possibility, the not-yet that destabilizes all concrete messianism, can be found in prophetic denunciations of social injustice as well in the cultured despair of the middle and upper classes and our withdrawal from political engagement. There is nothing that inevitably and irrevocably grounds our desire for justice. Justice, in all its forms, is our work, our creation, our unfinished task.

I. ALCHEMY

> *How exquisitely human was the wish for permanent happiness, and how thin human imagination became trying to achieve it.* [11]
>
> —TONI MORRISON, *Paradise*

How is it possible that all "manifestations" of the religious are amoral, if morality, if the demand for justice, is intrinsic to our names for the religious? For Lévinas, the name of God is a call for justice; for Derrida, the "*tout autre*" challenges the violence and fanaticism of any concrete messianism; for Irigaray and Jantzen, the imperative of the religious is to "become divine," which in itself is an act of justice, the open-ended participation in human flourishing.

I am not saying the religious is *immoral*, and thus, such names are, by definition, unwarranted. Rather the language of freedom and openness to others, the language of love and justice, coheres with ecstasy and claim of the religious as easily, but *no more easily*, than the language of exclusion and self-righteousness.

Another form of construing the sacred, found in feminist theology, process theology, and some African-American theologies is also instructive. Here the sacred is perceived as creativity itself. [12]

44

Let us think, though, about creativity. Creativity itself is as easily expressed in the operations of global capitalism, in the production of the music videos and websites, in the design and use of deadly weapons as it is in works of justice.[13] And, what feeds creativity? powerful connections with available human and natural resources. The work of scientists in Los Alamos constructing the first atomic weapons, for example, was a vivid manifestation of the power of human connection and creativity. The connections of the scientists at Los Alamos were, of course, partial. If they had been equally connected to the value of the people of Hiroshima and Nagasaki, if equally connected to the natural order, no such destructive weapons would have been built or used. And yet, could it be that the relative weakness of pacifist and prophetic movements in the face of military expansion and global capitalism is that *we are not as creative as* are they, from our vantage point in the ideal, are not as connected as are they to the actual human and natural resources of the world around us? If we ground our prophetic social critique in the "*tout autre*," do we then lack the creativity that comes from working with the resources that are here now? Injustice flourishes because those who love justice are singularly lacking in creativity, content to denounce the structures we see causing harm, inept in producing other forms of art, other economic structures, other political systems.

The experience of creativity, of intense forms of connection is simply this—the crucial synthesis of energies of people from the past, within the present, and even in the future. We may be energized, but that does not mean that our theological and political analyses are true, that our ethics and political strategies are just. It is disconcerting to acknowledge that our ecstasy in connection, whether political or conceptual, is simply the energy of connection, an energy that may be used in amoral, immoral, or moral ways. We so want the energy we experience in connection, the affirmation we encounter in "being-seen" or "being-loved" to be an affirmation of the rightness of our choices, actions, beliefs, and desires. While these may be affirmations of our being, they are not affirmations of how we frame and express that being.

What shape can imagination take, where is its thickness, its vitality if we are no longer constituted by the desire for perfection? What happens if we are no longer propelled by the goal of perfection and the sanction of a moral divine? What, then is the symbolics of desire, the symbolics of justice and creativity?

I'll describe a journey, one that begins with recognition of the ambiguity of our actions and then moves to an imagination that encompasses the amorality of the religious.

Theophus Smith describes the power of conjure in African-American religion. Conjure is the eliciting of spiritual power that transforms internalized oppression, and evokes and sustains acts of political transformation through a complex interaction of religious symbol systems, ritual performances and political action.[14] By definition, conjure escapes the dualistic oppositions of good and evil, sacred and profane. Working with Derrida's notion of the *pharmokos*, Smith claims that that which can heal can also harm.[15]

In some African religions and in the African-American religion of Vodou, Anthony Pinn claims that we find not only a recognition of the ambiguity of our own sacral activities but a recognition of the ambiguity of the divine. In his description of orisha service in the United States, the orishas are seen as "neutral energy forces affecting our lives," energy that "can be used for good or ill."[16] It is startling, to the western eye, to see a clear recognition of the amorality of the divine: ". . . [i]ndeed, there is no force in heaven which dictates a morality."[17]

If the forces that create and sustain us and the universe are amoral, what is the source of any particular moral vision? For there is a strong moral sense in orisha service, a morality that seeks to create and sustain a "proper relationship with the service, ancestors, other humans, and the earth."[18] We learn how to be moral not from God, not from a "being beyond being"—but from the experiences, teachings, and guidance conveyed to us by other human beings.[19]

What differentiates communal responses to constitutive energies? Our perception of these energies is socially constructed—the creation, and legacy, of our ancestors. Our mobilization of these energies is the creation of the interpretive communities in which we are formed. This energy can be used, and is used, for moral and political purposes: justifying our superiority and control of others, or, conversely, eliciting greater respect for and openness to others.

In her novels, Toni Morrison expresses this sensibility. In *Sula*, for example, she describes a nondualistic view of good and evil, and a clearly humanly-based rejection by African-Americans of violence and domination. The time frame of the novel is 1919–1965, a time of violent and systemic racism: lynching, mob violence, and harassment, legalized job discrimination, and segregation.

> What was taken by outsiders to be slackness, slovenliness, or even generosity was in fact a full recognition of the legitimacy of forces other than good ones . . . They did not believe Nature was ever askew — only inconvenient. Plague and drought were as "natural" as springtime. If milk could curdle, God knows robins could fall. The purpose of evil was to survive it and they determined (without ever knowing they had made up their minds to do it) to survive floods, white people, tuberculosis, famine, and ignorance. They knew anger well but not despair, and they didn't stone sinners for the same reason they didn't commit suicide — it was beneath them.[20]

Despair and violence were "beneath them": this is the gift of a communal legacy of resilience and respect, expressed as well by Patrick Chamoiseau in *Texaco*. Chamoiseau writes of those who knew "through which vices to rifle in order to stumble on virtue."[21] And, in so doing, we receive, we express a humanity of solicitude, tenderness, and dreams:

> I was surrounded by that solicitude which Quarters breed. I was given reinvigorating teas, hardy soups, bay rum rubs. I received nets of tenderness, cast seines full of dreams in which hands were held together . . . Each one of them tried to bring life back to my eyes.[22]

And, in return for this gift of solicitude, the protagonist of *Texaco*, Marie-Sophie, is able to give life to others:

> I had become something like the center of this resistance against the unrelenting beke. He took note of me himself. He came to me every day on errands of hate. The women handed me their swaddled misfortunes which I was unable to undo and which terrified me. All I had to do was look all-knowing, not wide-eyed before their fateful nonsense. And the little I would say to them would be enough to bring them back (for yet another moment) to the courage of living. That attitude gave the grave face and intense eyes men run away from.[23]

What brings us back "to the courage of living"? This is a matter of alchemy and desire. I see the religious not in terms of right belief and sure foundations, but as responses to amoral powers that can be given self-critically moral purposes. There are alchemical processes that have turned the bare bones of onto-theology into fierce, compassionate, and sustained movements for justice, and we can do the same.

II. AN A-THEOLOGY OF WONDER, SUFFERING, MEMORY, AND DESIRE

> *Lives don't make sense in reality, they come and go and often, like tsunamis, with the same crash, and they sweep away the dregs stagnating in your head like they were relics, which are treasures to you but don't stand still.*[24]
> —CHAMBOISEAU, *Texaco*

I write as one of the masses immersed fully in the wonder, pain, joy, fears, and hopes of the everyday. What is the religious symbolic, the poetics of desire that evokes meaning, that compels our work for

48

justice without desire for the transcendent, without desire for the "*tout autre*," without desire for "becoming divine"? I am an atheist, not just in the sense of the binary opposition of belief/unbelief, but in the sense of the symbolics of desire.[25] I write as one of those who does not desire God. We do not desire to become divine, but rather, we work to be human, "spirit and dust," and our prayers are venues opening us to our embeddedness in nature, in history, with all their peril and promise.[26] The horizon of our being is not "becoming divine," but being human, "vibrantly imperfect," attuned to the shifting forms of reciprocity between us and "all our relations."[27] At times we respond to the needs of vulnerable others, at times others respond to our vulnerability and our needs in an exchange that nourishes and sustains us, but cannot be calculated, predicted, nor controlled. Does anyone give more than infants and children? What love, delight, and awe they unleash in the worlds of those who respect them.[28]

I am dependent on the theological and political work of other feminists and womanists in a dual sense. Grounded in this work, I find untenable declarations of the impossibility of female subjectivity and agency.[29] We turn to the work and lives of the oppressed for a dual reason. Here there is not only an indictment of structures of bias, exclusion, and oppression, the legitimacy of religious traditions and social and political institutions challenged by lives shattered and voices broken, but construals of subjectivity, community, and agency that are partial *and* are powerful.[30] Womanist theologians and ethicists, for example, celebrate and analyze the life and work of all those, who though oppressed, have "made a way out of no way."[31]

There are two realities in the writings of many African-American and American Indian peoples: an indictment of the dominating alchemy given my culture's most precious and constitutive ideals, and, visions of subjectivity, agency, freedom, and community that resonate with the construction of self, desire, and world that I know. Patricia Williams, a critical legal theorist, uses the analogy of "alchemy" to describe the centuries-long process of giving political form to the ideals of equal rights, freedom, and justice.

> To say that blacks never fully believed in rights is true. Yet it is also true that blacks believed in them so much and so hard that we gave them life where there was none before . . . This was the resurrection of life from ashes four hundred years old. The making of something out of nothing took immense alchemical fire—the fusion of a whole nation and the kindling of several generations . . .[32]

The language of rights, the logic of divine justice, can be mobilized for justice, and can also be part of an alchemy of distance, isolation, and domination.[33]

Such a plethora of foundational "experiences" or encounters: a "god" who evokes love and justice, Schleiermacher's absolute dependence, Kierkegardian and Pauline "fear and trembling," Carol Christ's "great matrix of love," Tillichian "acceptance," Buber's "I and Thou," Derrida's "*tout autre*," Jantzen and Irigary's "becoming divine." How odd, how human, the impulse to reduce them to one, or to rank them, "ours" as the revelation, "theirs" as natural theology or mere human projection. What if the matter of the religious is far more complex, and far more diverse than can be reduced to any monism or any dualism of authentic/inauthentic, liberating/oppressive, freeing/reifying?[34] What all of these construals of the religious have in common is not any specific content, but their power, a power that is intrinsically ambiguous, the power of conjure, the power to heal and to harm.

WONDER

> *Say what you will, do what you will, life is not to be measured by the ell of its sorrows. For that reason, I, Marie-Sophie Laborieux, despite the river my eyes have shed, have always looked at the world in a good light. But how many wretched ones around me have choked the life out of their bodies? . . .*
>
> *But I never had these bad thoughts. With so many*

rags to launder in misery's rivers, I've never had time for melancholy. What's more, in the few moments life has left me, I learned to let my heart gallop on the saddle of intense feelings, to live life, as they say, to let her be. And note if you please that neither laughter nor smiles have ever tired the skin of my lips.

—CHAMBOISEAU, *Texaco*

Many long for the wholly other, yet we revel in the fully now. Our desire is the present in its abundance and wonder; our desire for justice a way of honoring the integrity of that which is, our political work an exuberant "virtuosity in the face of adversity."[35] This is not the religion of the "healthy-minded" criticized by William James, an unabashed embrace of life's pleasures and a resolute denial of life's horrors.[36] No, this is a passion, not for perfection, but for the "vibrantly imperfect" possible. It is not a passion for transgression, but a passion for the excess, the depth, the wonder, and the possibilities of the everyday. We work for justice with the tools of the present, and because of our love and respect for the present texture of lives. Not all is just, not all is honored, but that which is *valued* serves as the fulcrum from which to challenge all that devalues life. To us, it is the passion for the impossible that seems bereft, isolated from the beauty and vibrant connections that evoke respect and can be mobilized to work for justice.

As the quote from Chamboiseau makes clear, here we have a full awareness that life does destroy many people; injustice destroys lives and drives people mad. And yet, to again quote Chamboiseau: "To be part of it [City], I chose to act. And like the local youths say about politics around here: I chose battle over tears."[37]

Our passion is one of connection, open-eyed, and aware of the fragility of the matrix in which we live. Brock and Thistlethwaite describe a meditation on breath that can lead us to know the significance of these connections.

When we are trapped in the musings of our minds, wandering the temporal spheres of memory and future . . .

we are not fully in the present. When our whole being is fully attuned to the present, . . . enormous energy and life are unleashed. The discipline of learning to breathe in such restorative ways comes in community with others who breathe . . . In this breathing together we can inspire each other with grace and compassion to conspire for change.[38]

Being in the present can bring stasis and closure. Being in the present may also open us, connect us, and empower us with dynamic fullness. As Chamboiseau states, "draw in excess from those you love."[39]

What we draw "from those we love" can be described, but not trapped in definitive formulations, in truths that can be reflected in the logic of belief/unbelief. Leslie Marmon Silko, for example, describes the truths that are communal, the legacy of the people of the Laguna Pueblo, truths whose meaning is intrinsically open and multifaceted:

> Communal storytelling was a self-correcting process in which listeners were encouraged to speak up if they noted an important fact or detail omitted. The people were happy to listen to two or three different versions of the same event . . . . The ancient Pueblo people sought a communal truth, not an absolute. For them this truth lived somewhere within the web of differing versions, disputes over minor points, outright contradictions tangling with old feuds and village rivalries.[40]

This "living truth" is a truth of engagement and desire, a way of being in a world we can never fully understand, not a metaphysics of how things really are.[41]

This is not a story with an end, although it is a story with many meanings. It is an engagement with life, and a passion for its wealth. It is not hope for an end, for a lasting resolution. It is not a longing for the totally new nor is it the expectation of the repetition of the same, the endless return of the known and the expected. Morrison writes of our desire for, our solace in, the rhythms of the present, their openness and their resonance:

In ocean hush a woman black as firewood is singing. Next to her is a younger woman whose head rests on the singing woman's lap. . . .

There is nothing to beat this solace which is what Piedade's song is about, although the words evoke memories neither one has ever had: of reaching age in the company of the other; of speech shared and divided bread smoking from the fire; the unambivalent bliss of going home to be at home— the ease of coming back to love begun. When the oceans heave sending rhythms of water ashore, Piedade looks to see what has come. Another ship, perhaps, but different, heading to port, crew and passengers, lost and saved, atremble, for they have been disconsolate for some time. Now they will rest before shouldering the endless work they were created to do down here in Paradise.[42]

Memory/Generations

> *Write* The Word? *No. But tie the knot with life again, yes.*[43]
>
> —Chamboiseau, *Texaco*

Ours is not the desire of becoming divine. It is the passion of "shouldering the endless work" in "Paradise," of tying the knot with life again. We "tie the knot" not because of master narratives of destiny and promise, of resolution won, but we live out of the threads of connection, the threads of recognition within which we come to life. Chamboiseau recounts a tale of persistent work in face of defeat:

> I wanted to show strength, and so never . . . would I stand round taking pity on my fate like I so often felt like doing. . . . Under the dull eyes of the others, I lifted my poles back up, straightened my partitions, spread my oilcloths . . . and my tears drowned in my sweat. The others looked at me for a

long time, then, one by one, the women went back to their own wreckage.[44]

How do we gain the will to continue, to let "our tears drown in our sweat"? This persistent affirmation of life does not emerge from an exercise of will; it is not the result of our reason, it is, rather, the gift, the legacy, of generations.

Brock and Thistlethewaite point to the fragility of "truth" and the need of a social movement to hold the "truths" of compassion and commitment.[45] This "holding" is communal and generational, a form of power expressed through its fragility and not in spite of it. This power of generations is described well by Kasimu and Karen Baker-Fletcher. In their systematic theology, they add another category to the well-known list of eschatology, ecclesiology, christology, anthropology, and doctrine of God. They speak of generations: the collective matrix of our being; past which engendered us, the present and future we engender. They cite the cosmological community principle *muntu*, of the Bantu peoples of Southeastern Africa: "I am because We are; and We are because I am."[46]

> On a plantation, on a slave ship, on a farm, in the city, in the suburbs, in the church, in a mosque, in the wilderness— we have found and must continue to find ways to carve our sacred time and space to pass on tools of wisdom and survival to our children, our children's children, and one another.[47]

Karen and Kasimu Baker-Fletcher also remind us that "generations must not be romanticized": "[w]hen we idealize the elders we learn far less of what life has taught them or can teach us than if we learn from their strengths and their weaknesses."[48]

This legacy of virtuosity, of living fully in the "vibrantly imperfect" possible, is described as well by Leslie Marmon Silko. She sees this as the gift of Laguna story telling, an oral tradition that recounts even "disturbing or provocative" events.

The effect of these inter-family or inter-clan exchanges is the reassurance of each person that she or he will never be separated or apart from the claxclan. Neither the worst blunders or disasters nor the greatest financial prosperity and joy will ever be permitted to isolate anyone from the rest of the group.... You are never the first to suffer a grave loss or profound humiliation. You are never the first, and you understand that you will probably not be the last to commit or be victimized by a repugnant act.[49]

We are not the first to suffer and fail, and we will not be the last. We are not the first to also embody a measure of justice, and we will not be the last.

To see the world through the lenses of compassion and empathy, to create our world with this passion for life affirming justice, is not a duty, a demand, an obligation, or a sacrifice. It is, rather, a blessing and a gift. This life of seeking justice does have costs, but the ability to respect others enough to have a passion for justice, the ability to mourn and rage our own suffering and that of others, is not an onerous task, but a rich legacy. Its source is not our own achievement, but the gift of generations who shaped us, the ancestors who gave ethical and aesthetic form to the energy of life.[50]

This symbolic of religion has, at its core, horror and rage at injustice and a fierce longing for justice, for personal and individual institutions that embody respect.

What do we mean by justice? What is the criteria for our work? Respect for the other. Patricia Williams claims that if we respect each other, we "give to all of society's objects and untouchables the rights of privacy, integrity, and self-assertion; [we] give them distance and respect."[51] Carol Lee Sanchez describes the respect at the core of the traditions of people of the Laguna Pueblo, recognizing the integrity of "all my relations," human, natural, animal, and the dynamic balance that can exist between all of us.[52] This is not the vulnerable face of Lévinas, but the compelling "you" of Buber's I-You relationship.[53] Lévinas describes a way some people see otherness, as threat, as vulnerable, as demand, he tries to limit the violence against that other.[54] Within the work of feminist, womanist, and liberation theologians, we see, however, a basically different reception of otherness.[55] At its core, there is reciprocity. This reciprocity is expressed in Chamboiseau's description of building the Quarters:

> I was piling up all these things by my hutch, waiting for a hand.
> If someone gives you a hand, you have to stand ready with at least one canari of vegetables, with a piece of cod, a gallon of rum, glasses and madou. Once I was ready, I rang out the call . . . Then things went very fast. My hutch attracted other hutches . . . The very people on the slope lent a helping hand, gave advice, helped, shouldered each other.[56]

This is not caring for the vulnerable other. Nor is this reciprocity calculated, or constrained. It is, rather, the exuberant expression of mutuality.

Many of us cannot see the other, the face, the way Lévinas does. Our alternative seeing, one of curiosity and respect, is not a choice, but the gift of the ancestors. We see as we were seen; we love as we were loved.

What would it mean for our political organizing if we began with the premise that our passion for justice is not our achievement, but a gift? What if we realized that caring about injustice is not the result of our astute socio-political analyses, our compassion, our courage, and our will, but the result of being loved, recognized, and seen by others? Longing for justice, mourning and raging in the face of injustice is the gift of the ancestors; it is the gift of "all our relations." What would it mean if we focused on the blessing of respect? I do not know, but I want to find out.[57]

I know that this recognition does call us away from prophetic denunciation of the hard and close-mindedness of others. It calls us from any satisfaction in merely denouncing structures and peoples who exploit or ignore others. When we acknowledge the strength and dignity of others, when we empathize with the suffering of others, when we cast our lot in acts of creating justice, our selves are enlarged by the blessing of openness, the blessing of an open heart, and the blessing of an enlivened imagination.

CONCLUSION

What then, is the religious? This is the name we give to those encounters, those energies, which are constitutive, but amoral; those encounters, those energies which are vivid, compelling and meaningful, but fragile. This symbolic of desire is not better than other construals of the religious, for it has its own peril and promise.[58] It does lead to justice and it can also sustain structures of isolation and domination. I am not as aware of the fundamental, constitutive dangers of this logic as I would I like to be, but I can identify four. One of the greatest dangers is complacency: if we are relatively safe and comfortable, removed from the immediate costs of oppression, it is easy to relish the beauty of life and leave the work of building justice to those who are suffering direct injustice.

Another constitutive danger is settling for too little. If one forgoes the illusion of utopia, and chooses instead "connections that are real and hopes that are realizable," we may settle for reforms that are less far-reaching than is actually possible.[59] There is an element of madness, folly, and excess in any work for justice: an exuberant overreaching of the limits of the present. Embedded as we are in complex networks of other actors, with other hopes and desires, we cannot tell the difference between what we can change and what we cannot. We cannot tell in advance of the struggle if we will succeed or fail; we cannot predict the ramifications of our actions in the present or the future. Our wager is more audacious: what improbable task, with which unfathomable and unpredictable results shall we undertake today?

Another constitutive risk, one true of any construal of the religious that valorizes religious ecstasy and the intensity of religious experience, is that this mysticism, or this intense connection to other people, separates us from life and leads us to have disdain for "ordinary" life and "ordinary" people, who supposedly, do not know this ecstatic connection. The dangers are twofold: it is often difficult to translate the ecstasy of mystical experiences into the possibilities and demands of daily life. Rather than mysticism being a way of "illumining the everyday;" it can be an escape from the everyday, or construed as more than the material, more valuable than the daily tasks of life.[60] These intense experiences and connections can also lead to disdain for other people. If this sense of connection and energy seems new to us, and our prior life seems meaningless or shallow in contrast to what we now know, we may project our prior meaninglessness onto others, assuming, to quote the camp song, that we know a love, a peace, a joy "that the world does not know."

In her novel *Paradise*, Morrison recounts the tragedy of a town that in escaping slavery and exclusion, defined itself as exclusive, and violently so, a town that in trying to give its youth safety, denied their vitality and creativity. *Even the energy of generations is amoral*: it can be used to stifle and bind, rather than to frame and nourish.

> How exquisitely human was the wish for permanent happiness, and how thin human imagination became trying to achieve it. Soon Ruby will be like any other country town: the young thinking of elsewhere; the old full of regret. The sermons will be eloquent but fewer and fewer will pay attention or connect them to everyday life. How can they hold it together, he wondered, this hard-won heaven defined only by the absence of the unsaved, the unworthy and the strange? Who will protect them from their leaders?[61]

How can we acknowledge that there is no fundamental divide of us the righteous, us the vanguard, us the enlightened, and the "unsaved, the unworthy and the strange?" We can "return to laughter," learning from the stranger within and the stranger outside, blessed with the legacy of seeing all as worthy of dignity, privacy and respect.[62] We can return to laughter, the generous laughter that relishes the irony of knowing that that which funds our morality is itself amoral, and morality, far from being the demand or gift of the divine, is the perilous and at times beautiful human response to the energy and wonder of life.

AUTHOR'S NOTE

Return to Laughter is an anthropological novel written by Laura Bohannen under the pseudonym of Elenore Smith Bowen, and first published in 1954. Bohannen, an American anthropologist, describes her attempts to "objectively" study tribal peoples in Nigeria. Bohannen describes the breakdown of her conviction of cultural superiority, from her initial arrogant impatience with education into the names of different plants, to her discovery of a communal social logic of rage, laughter, forgiveness and intensity that proved more resilient in the face of social crisis than her own dualistic moral vocabulary of good and evil, friend and foe.

NOTES

---

[1] Jean-Luc Marion, *God Without Being* (Chicago: University of Chicago Press, 1991).

[2] Grace Jantzen provides a philosophy of religion from a feminist perspective. Building on the work of Luce Irigaray, she develops a new imaginary of religion, a feminist symbolic of natality and flourishing to replace a masculinist symbolic of death. In so doing, her focus is on a symbolics of desire and not the justification of belief: "What might happen, then, if we were to relinquish the preoccupation with the rational justification of belief and the evaluation of truth-claims and try to follow the path of desire to/for the divine?" (p. 65).

In this essay I follow Grace Jantzen and the recasting of the philosophy of religion in terms of the "opening of desire" and not the insistence on
belief; and hence, the "centrality of evidence argument, counter-argument,
and so on." "But once we note that this is the case for either pole of the binary, then a gap opens up, a possibility of thinking differently, and asking
whether, instead of this insistence upon belief, we might focus on other possibilities—love, for example, or longing, or desire . . . what if instead we were
to explore . . . the opening of desire that interrupts this emphasis on belief
with longing for the divine horizon?" p. 65 and chapter 4. Grace Jantzen,
Becoming Divine: Towards a Feminist Philosophy of Religion (Bloomington:
Indiana University Press, 1999).

[3] Thee Smith, "W/Riting Black Theology," *Forum* 5: 4 (December 1980),
pp. 50–51.

[4] For a representative critique of the claims of metaphysical theology and
the methods of ontotheology, see Grace Jantzen, *Becoming Divine*; Philippa
Berry and Andrew Wernick, *Shadow of Spirit: Postmodernism and Religion*
(London and New York: Routledge, 1992); Paul Lakeland, *Postmodernity:
Christian Identity in a Fragmented Age* (Minneapolis: Fortress Press, 1997).

[5] Jantzen, *Becoming Divine*, p. 97.

[6] "Religion marks the place of the absolute *for us*, its path, the hope of its
fulfillment. All too often that fulfillment has been postponed or transferred
to some transcendental time and place. It has not been interpreted as the
infinite that resides within us and among us, the god in us, the Other for us,
becoming with and in us . . . This God, are we capable of imagining it as a
woman? Can we dimly see it as the perfection of our subjectivity?" Luce
Irigaray, *Sexes and Genealogies*, trans. Gillian C. Gill (New York: Columbia
University Press, 1993), p. 63.

[7] Sharon D. Welch, *A Feminist Ethic of Risk* (Minneapolis: Fortress Press,
1990).

[8] Karl Barth, "The Question of Natural Theology," pp. 49–86 in *Church
Dogmatics: A Selection*, selected and with an introduction by Helmut
Gollwitzer, translated and edited by G. W. Brorniley (New York: Harper,
1962). See, also, Derrida's contrast between legitimate and illegitimate forms
of messianic expectation: "Now, if there is a spirit of Marxism which I will

never be ready to renounce, it is not only the critical idea or the questioning stance (a consistent deconstruction must insist on them even as it also learns that this is not the last or first word). It is even more a certain emancipatory and *messianic* affirmation, a certain experience of the promise that one can try to liberate from any dogmatics and even from any metaphysico-religious determination, from any *messianism*. And a promise must promise to be kept, that is, not to remain 'spiritual' or 'abstract,' but to produce events, new effective forms of action, practice, organization, and so forth" (p. 89). *Specters of Marx: The State of the Debt, the Work of Mourning, and the New International*, trans. Peggy Kamug Kamuf (New York: Routledge, 1994). See also John D. Caputo's thorough discussion of the critique of concrete messianism, religious violence and coercion in *The Prayers and Tears of Jacques Derrida: Religion Without Religion* (Bloomington: Indiana University Press, 1997), introduction, chapter 3, and conclusion.

[9] Jacques Derrida, *The Gift of Death*, trans. David Willis (Chicago: University of Chicago Press). See also Caputo's exploration of the theological and philosophical significance of Derrida's thought, *The Prayers and Tears of Jacques Derrida*; Emmanuel Lévinas, *Basic Philosophical Writings*, ed. Adriaan T. Peperzak, Simon Critchley, and Robert Bernasconi (Bloomington: Indiana University Press, 1996), p. 29.

[10] Nietzsche, *Twilight of the Idols, or, How One Philosophizes With a Hammer*, trans. Richard Polt (Indianapolis, Indiana: Hackett, 1997).

[11] Toni Morrison, *Paradise* (New York: Alfred A. Knopf, 1998), p. 306.

[12] Karen Baker-Fletcher and Garth Kasimu Baker-Fletcher, *My Sister, My Brother: Womanist and Xodus God-Talk* (Maryknoll, N.Y.: Orbis, 1997), p. 180; see also Birch and Cobb's discussion of trusting "life as the creative good" (p. 180). Charles Birch and John B. Cobb, Jr., *The Liberation of Life: From the Cell to the Community* (Cambridge: Cambridge University Press, 1981).

[13] Rosabeth Moss Kanter extols the creativity of global capitalism, and argues that it is fed by the skills and worldviews of "cosmopolitans": "Cosmopolitans are rich in three intangible assets . . . that translate into pre-eminence and power in a global economy: concepts—the best and latest knowledge and ideas; competence—the ability to operate at the highest standards of any place anywhere; and connections—the best relationships,

which provide access to the resources of other people and organizations around the world." Rosabeth Moss Kanter, *World Class: Thriving Locally in the Global Economy* (New York: Simon and Schuster, 1995), p. 23.

[14] Theophus Smith, *Conjuring Culture: Biblical Formations of Black America* (Oxford: Oxford University Press, 1994), pp. 3–12, 18. Smith's understanding of "conjure" is different in emphasis from that of Derrida in Specters of Marx. Derrida also refers to "conjuration" as "the appeal that causes to come forth . . . what is not there at the present moment of the appeal" (p. 41). Yet his focus is on conjure as exorcism, the "destruction" and "disavowal" of a "malignant, demonized, diabolized force" (p. 48). Smith's "conjure" is performative and creative: the evocation of freedom, of particular forms of life, and not primarily "certifying death" (Derrida, *Gift of Death*, p. 48).

[15] Smith, *Conjuring Culture*, pp. 31, 43; Jacques Derrida, "Plato's Pharmacy," in *Dissemination* trans. Barbara Johnson (Chicago: University of Chicago Press, 1981).

[16] Anthony B. Pinn, *Varieties of African American Religious Experience* (Minneapolis: Fortress Press, 1998), p. 101.

[17] Ibid., p. 102.

[18] Ibid., p. 72. See also the work of Karen McCarthy Brown for a thorough exploration of the moral sense of Haitian Vodou: Karen McCarthy Brown, "Alourdes: A Case Study of Moral Leadership in Haitian Vodou," in *Saints and Virtues*, ed. John Hawley (Berkeley: University of California Press, 1987); Karen McCarthy Brown, *Mama Lola: A Vodou Priestess in Brooklyn* (Berkeley: University of California Press, 1991).

[19] Pinn, *Varieties of African American Religious Experience*, p. 102. See also Charles Long's discussion of the role of interpretive communities in *Significations*.

[20] Toni Morrison, *Sula* (New York: Bantam, 1973), p. 90.

[21] In *Texaco*, the winner of the Prix Goncourt, Patrick Chamoiseau traces one hundred and fifty years of post-slavery Caribbean history, told from the perspective of Marie-Sophie Laborieux, the daughter of a slave, who leads in the establishment of a shantytown on the outskirts of a Caribbean city.

Patrick Chamoiseau, *Texaco*, translated from the French and Creole by Rose-Myriarn Rejouis and Val Vinokurov (New York: Pantheon Books, 1997), p. 119.

22 Ibid., pp. 263–264.

23 Ibid., p. 341.

24 Ibid., p. 310.

25 Jantzen argues that "it would be more accurate to see atheism/theism not as itself the relevantly significant binary, but as one *pole* of a binary, the repressed other being every thing else which is unacknowledged in the centrality of this pair" (p. 65). Jantzen claims that "the repressed other" is the "opening of desire that interrupts this emphasis on belief" (p. 65). Following Irigaray, she looks for a "new morning of the world," "developing a feminist philosophy of religion whose founding gesture is not the justification of beliefs which separates the "true" from the "false," but rather an imaginative longing for the divine in a reduplication of desire not content with the old gods but seeking the horizon and the foundation needed to progress between past and future" (Irigaray). Jantzen, *Becoming Divine*, p. 99.

26 This is an atheistic version of the theistic symbolic of "spirit and dust" developed by Karen Baker-Fletcher in *Sisters of Dust, Sisters of Spirit: Womanist Wordings on God and Creation* (Minneapolis: Fortress Press. 1998). The "atheism" highlights our acceptance of finitude and imperfection. I agree with Jantzen's symbolic of natality, but think the force of our full affirmation of finitude is clearer if we relinquish Irigaray's symbolic of perfection and Jantzen's symbolic of becoming divine. It is important to note however, that for Jantzen, "becoming divine" does not mean that finitude is devalued: "A symbolic of natality is not in any sense a denial of death or a pretense that death does not matter" (p. 152). "The acceptance of life is an acceptance of limits, which, after all, enable as much as they constrain: the boundless is beyond capacity. The obligation to become divine is not an obligation to become limitless; the quest for infinity would be a renunciation, not a fulfillment, of our gendered, embodied selves" (p. 154). "Rather than squander our energy in a futile struggle against finitude, we can rejoice in the (limited) life we have as natals and act for love of the world" (p. 155).

[27] In our affirmation of the present and the everyday, we address the critique voiced by Rieder: "For some time now, the cultural left has been going around in a funk, deconstructing everything in sight, wavering between scolding a culture that seems hostile to liberation and conducting a promiscuous search for signs of resistance to that culture's dominating symbols. But in all this rage for representation, the left has often committed soul murder too, projecting disappointment onto the objects of its gaze, representing itself rather than the complex reality of a vibrantly imperfect culture." Jonathan Rieder, *New York Times Book Review*, December 26, 1998, p. 15.

[28] Cynthia Willett, for example, contrasts a patriarchal (and elitist) symbolic of self and desire with resources for self, community, freedom, and desire seen in African American experience and in the mother-child interaction. She describes the sensually mediated logic of intersubjectivity found in the writing of Frederick Douglass, who evoked the power of the touch of his mother and grandmother to create a self correlated with community and openness (pp. 8, 170). She also turns to Daniel Stem and the analysis of the activity of the infant in relationship to the mother to show the limits of views that see this experience as inchoate and passive, as either one-sided or amorphous and prior to meaning, meaning occurring only through the phallic intervention of language (pp. 24, 43, 47). Cynthia Willett, *Maternal Ethics and Other Slave Moralities* (New York: Routledge, 1995).

[29] Irigaray claims that "[t]he (male) ideal other has been imposed upon women by men. Man is supposedly woman's more perfect other, her model, her essence. The most human and the most divine goal woman can conceive is to become man. If she is to become woman, if she is to accomplish her female subjectivity, woman needs a god who is a figure for the perfection of her subjectivity. *Sexes and Genealogies*, p. 64.

[30] Iris Marion Young describes five faces of oppression and their constraints on agency and subjectivity in *Justice and the Politics of Difference* (Princeton: Princeton University Press, 1990).

[31] Central to the work of womanist theologians and ethicists is the recognition that these limits have not completely shaped the agency and subjectivity of people of color. D. Soyini Madison, for example, begins her collection of writings by women of color, by explaining the significance of this saying: "I remember my mother standing, in 'colored woman' style, her arms akimbo and her head tilted to the side, speaking quietly but forcefully in a tone

that could scare a bull. She would willfully declare: 'Being the woman that I am I will make a way out of no way.' These were *mother's* words, but they are also the words and the will of all women of color who assert who they are, who create sound out of silence, and who build worlds out of remnants ... *The Woman That I Am* is a proclamation of the 'I' in each individual woman's identity, but it is also a testament to the collective power of women of color," p. 1. *The Woman That I Am: The Literature and Culture of Contemporary Women of Color* (New York: St. Martin's Press, 1994).

As an example of womanist theology and ethics, see also the works of Karen Baker-Fletcher; Emilie M. Townes, *In A Blaze of Glory: Womanist Spirituality As Social Witness* (Nashville: Abingdon Press, 1995) Emilie M. Townes, ed., *Embracing the Spirit: Womanist Perspectives on Hope, Salvation and Transformation* (Maryknoll, N.Y.: Orbis Books, 1997); Katie G. Cannon, *Black Womanist Ethics* (Atlanta: Scholars Press, 1988); Delores Williams, *Sisters in the Wilderness: The Challenge of Womanist God-Talk* (Maryknoll, N.Y.: Orbis, 1993).

[32] Patricia J. Williams, *The Alchemy of Race and Rights: Diary of Law Professor* (Cambridge, Mass.: Harvard University Press, 1991), p. 163.

[33] Philip Arnold describes the way the language of "utopia" justified the "complete annihilation of indigenous people": "the hope of a technological utopian dream was expressed at the 1892 Columbian Exposition in Chicago. At this World's Fair and those that followed, Lakota people specifically, and indigenous people from around the world more generally, were presented as the clear and identifiable impediments to a modern view of progress" (p. 94). In the writing of L. Frank Baum (later the author of *The Wonderful Wizard of Oz*), there was the explicit claim that "the realization of this utopian dream ... required the complete annihilation of indigenous people, ... in order to protect our civilization" (p. 88); Philip Arnold, "Black Elk and Book Culture," *Journal of the American Academy of Religion* 67:1 (March 1999).

[34] For an alternative examination of the significance of the diversity of religious experience, see Laurel C. Schneider, *Re-Imaging the Divine: Confronting the Backlash against Feminist Theology* (Cleveland: Pilgrim Press, 1998). Schneider argues for a monistic polytheism that "lends authority and legitimacy to revelatory religious experience in all of its diversity" (p. 175). Where I differ, fundamentally, from Schneider's thought-provoking proposal is her use of metaphors of divine certainty, finality, power, and goodness.

35 Chamboiseau, *Texaco*, p. 33.

36 Eric Lott uses this metaphor to describe the artistic power of the jazz musician Charlie Parker: "Jazz was a struggle which pitted mind against the perversity of circumstance, and . . . in this struggle blinding virtuosity was the best weapon." "Double V, Double-Time: Bebop's Politics of Style," in *Jazz Among the Discourses*, ed. Krin Gabbard (Durham: Duke University Press, 1995), p. 243.

37 William James, *The Varieties of Religious Experience* (Cambridge, Mass.: Harvard University Press, 1985). James's critique of "healthy-mindedness" is found in lectures four and five. These lectures were delivered as the Gifford Lectures on Natural Religion at Edinburgh University in 1901 and 1902.

38 Chamboiseau, *Texaco*, p. 34

39 Rita Nakashima Brock and Susan Brooks Thistlethwaite, *Casting Stones: Prostitution and Liberation in Asia and the United States* (Minneapolis: Fortress Press, 1996), p. 279.

40 Leslie Marmon Silko, "Landscape, History and the Pueblo Imagination," in *The Woman that I Am*, ed. D. Soyini Madison, p. 502.

41 Ibid., p. 499.

42 Morrison, *Paradise*, p. 318.

43 Chamboiseau, *Texaco*, p. 294.

44 Ibid., p. 340.

45 Brock and Thistlethwaite, *Casting Stones*, p. 279.

46 Karen and Kasimu Baker-Fletcher, *My Sister, My Brother*, pp. 203–204.

47 Ibid., p. 178.

48 Ibid., pp. 178, 184.

49 Silko, "Landscape, History and the Pueblo Imagination," p. 506.

[50] Pinn, *Varieties of African American Religious Experience*, pp. 101–102.

[51] Patricia Williams, *The Alchemy of Race and Rights*, p. 165.

[52] Carol Lee Sanchez is a native New Mexican of Laguna Pueblo, Lakota, and Lebanese heritage. She states that "the most fundamental meaning of the word *Sacred* for Native Americans is 'entitled to reverence and respect' ... American Indians believe the universe and everything in it is 'entitled to reverence and respect'.... Thus the Tribal Principle of Relationship, that we are all related, is a natural extension of this belief. The Tribes teach that when we are disrespectful, irreverent, or abusive to the inhabitants of our environment, they will abandon us" (p. 224). Attention to "all our relations," human, animal, plant, and mineral, is the ground of living a good life, or "walking in Beauty." If we pay attention to "all our relations," we see where we are abusive and out of balance, and we gain insight in how harmony and balance may be restored (p. 211). "Animal, Vegetable, and Mineral," in *Ecofeminism and the Sacred*, ed. Carol J. Adams (New York: Continuum, 1994), pp. 207–228.

[53] Martin Buber, *I and Thou*, (New York: Charles Scribner's Sons, 1970).

[54] See Jantzen's thorough critique of Lévinas reification of the "vulnerable" face: "What sort of symbolic does it bespeak and reinforce if the most insistent thing that comes to mind in being face to face with the Other is the desire to kill? Even granting that this is what Lévinas sees as the violent logic of western ontology, in which mastery is the founding gesture and killing is its logical conclusion, to speak of this in terms of individual desire and temptation is shocking ... Why the impulse to kill? Why not, say, an impulse to smile, or feed, or kiss, or converse? Why the assumed hostility, what Lévinas later writes of as 'the face of the neighbor in its persecuting hatred'? ... Could he say what he does if the face which confronts him is the face of an infant? a mother? one natal greeting another?" (p. 239). See also pages 237–253. Jantzen, *Becoming Divine*.

[55] For feminist and womanist explorations of mutuality and reciprocity, see, for example, Rosemary Radford Ruether, *Women and Redemption: A Theological History* (Minneapolis: Fortress Press, 1998); Rosemary Radford Ruether, *Gaia and God: An Ecofentinist Theology of Earth Healing* (San Francisco: HarperSanFrancisco, 1992); Carter Heyward, *Touching Our Strength: The Erotic as Power and the Love of God* (San Francisco: Harper and

Row, 1989); Catherine Keller, *From a Broken Web: Separation, Sexism and Self* (Boston: Beacon, 1986); Chung Hyun Kyung, *Struggle to be the Sun Again: Introducing Asian Women's Theology* (Maryknoll, N.Y.: Orbis, 1990); Ada Mariá Isási-Diáz, *Mujerista Theology* (Maryknoll, N.Y.: Orbis, 1997); Rebecca Chopp, *The Power to Speak: Feminism, Language, God* (New York: Crossroad, 1989); Mary Daly, *Gyn/Ecology: The Metaethics of Radical Feminism* (Boston: Beacon Press 1985); Paula Cooey, *Religious Imagination and the Body: A Feminist Analysis* (New York: Oxford University Press, 1994); Rita Nakashima Brock, *Journeys by Heart: A Christology of Erotic Power* (New York: Crossroad, 1991); Sallie McFague, *The Body of God: An Ecological Theology* (Minneapolis: Fortress Press, 1993).

[56] Chamnsboiseau, *Texaco*, p. 300.

[57] I have been an activist in left and feminist politics all of my adult life. This is not the attitude that fueled our protests, our demands for social justice and our denunciations of oppressive institutions and individuals.

[58] I have followed here the example set by Roger S. Gottlieheb in "The Transcendence of Justice and the Justice of Transcendence: Mysticism, Deep Ecology and Political Life," *Journal of the American Academy of Religion*, 67:1 (March 1999), pp. 149–166. Gottlieb disavows any metaphysical grounding for his vision of mysticism, describes the mysticism of "deep ecology" clearly, and yet describes what he sees as four intrinsic dangers of this form of mysticism.

[59] Pinn, *Varieties of African American Religious Experience*, p. 184.

[60] "The vision of mysticism offered here will not satisfy everyone. It is a particularly non-metaphysical view in which ultimate reality is pretty much exhausted by 'ordinary' reality. Of course, when illuminated by the sparks of mystical experience, 'ordinary' reality can shine quite brightly, as in the old Zen story that identifies true enlightenment with simply seeing 'a mountain as a mountain and a river as a river." Gottleib, "Transcendence of Justice and the Justice of Transcendence," p. 164.

[61] Morrison, *Paradise*, p. 306. For another discussion of the importance of generational connections, and yet a recognition of the oppressive potential and actuality of those connections, see Isási-Diáz, *Mujerista Theology*, pp. 137–144.

62 "They knew how to live at close quarters with tragedy, how to live with their own failure and yet laugh. They knew the terror of a broken society, where brother's hand is raised against brother in hate and fear; they knew how to come back, brother to brother, and create life anew . . . those people . . . who all know they may themselves be faithless and crippled, and who all know that they build on shifting sand, have yet the courage to build what they know will fall . . . It is the laughter of people who value love and friend-ship and plenty, who have lived with terror and death and hate." Elenore Smith Bowen, *Return to Laughter: An Anthropological Novel* (New York: Anchor Books, 1964), p. 297.

New Words for Life

Thandeka

Unitarian Universalist General Assembly
Boston, Massachusetts
June 27, 2003

U nitarian Universalists need a new language of reverence
to solve a current problem. Presently, we affirm two
conflicting doctrines of human nature. One doctrine is
a legacy of the man who gave American Unitarianism a "party
platform," William Ellery Channing (Wright, 3). Channing said
our human essence is the mind, which he believed was independent from the body. The other doctrine is a legacy of Universalism's
singularly important nineteenth-century leader, Hosea Ballou, who
said our human essence is the mind and the body, which together
define and determine our experiences. When our two historic
traditions consolidated in 1961 we ended up with one religion,
Unitarian Universalism, which affirms two incompatible doctrines
of human nature. A new language of reverence enables us to resolve
this problem.

Currently, the doctrinal problem prevents us from talking coherently about who we are as a religious people. Unitarian
Universalism, as part of a wider, liberal theological tradition,
begins with a set of assumptions about human nature rather than
with doctrinal claims about God, scripture, revelation, or church
tradition. If our assumptions about human nature do not cohere,

then the theology that articulates them will not cohere either. This is the state in which we find ourselves today.

No one is more aware of the fallout from this problem than our children. They grow up and leave our church because they find little within it that makes sense or sustains them. And so our congregations survive as the church of strangers, the place for dissidents who have left their original traditions for doctrinal reasons and for those who seek a religious tradition in which indefinition is its defining attraction.

Our visitors are also aware of this problem. Five out of seven people who visit our churches do not return. We can do better than this. We *must* to better than this. We—and our children—need a church that enlivens and sustains us all. So, too, does our world.

We begin this new work by resolving the historical debate between Channing and Ballou.[1]

THE UNFINISHED DEBATE

The debate between Channing and Ballou began with the 1832 publication of Channing's "The Evil of Sin." In it, Channing attacked Hosea Ballou's Universalist claim that sinners are not punished after they die for the moral sins they committed while on earth. Channing also explained his own doctrine, one of future retribution for human beings in the afterlife: "The miseries of disobedience to conscience and God are not exhausted in this life. Sin deserves, calls for, and will bring down future, greater misery. This Christianity teaches, and this nature teaches" (Channing, 221). Both revelation and religious truths taught by human reason and conscience, Channing insisted, affirmed his doctrine of sin and salvation. He relied on two distinct sources for evidence to support his claims: Christian doctrine based on divine revelation and Christian doctrine known and affirmed through human reason and conscience (human nature).

Ballou responded a year later in his essay "A Candid Examination of Dr. Channing's Discourse on the Evil of Sin." Ballou first pointed out the internal contradictions in Channing's arguments, the unsupported assertions and the counterbiblical assumptions. Channing's "doctrine of an unmerciful retribution, in the world to come, for sins committed in this moral state," Ballou concluded, "gives our Creator the very worst character that the human mind can conceive. It is atheism, gross atheism, to pretend that such a state of suffering can exist, without allowing that its existence was originally embraced in the vast scheme of the divine purpose" (Ballou, 29). For suffering to follow resurrection, Ballou reasoned, sin would also follow resurrection, as suffering results from sin. This means that Christ's suffering and death would have been for naught.

To bring his own set of theological points home, Ballou presented an image of what carrying sin into the future life would look like:

> A picture more appalling, more withering to virtuous hope, and blasting to the aspirations of mercy and compassion, was never drawn. Angels of mercy, deliver us from a fiend that would blot out the sun, the moon, and the stars, and destroy every beauty and all the loveliness of creation, but preserve sin with maternal fondness! Had [Channing's] eye but caught a glimpse of this haggard form, his affectionate heart, his benevolent soul would have frozen (Ballou, 15).

Ballou next turned to a critique of Channing's doctrine of human nature to answer a new question: Why hadn't Channing's heart glimpsed this haggard form? To answer this question, Ballou added an appendix to his discourse. In it he investigated Channing's doctrine of human nature and concluded that Channing believed the mind of man is independent from its body, is capable of existing without it, and, after death, creates a new body for itself (Ballou, 33–34; Channing, 227).

After reviewing these claims, Ballou concluded that, according to Channing, the mind is not part of the body. The mind simply uses the body to accomplish its own mental desires. Channing,

Ballou insisted, "believes that all moral evil, all vice or wrongdoing in which men have ever employed their mental or physical powers originated not from the body.... [Rather, the mind simply] uses the several parts and the members of the body as mere instruments convenient for accomplishing its own evil purposes." Channing, we might say, espoused a doctrine that in contemporary terms could be called a doctrine of a split self: a mind at war with its body's own self-acknowledged sentiments.

Astonished by this bifurcated doctrine of human nature, Ballou asked rhetorically, "What desire ever influenced the will to an evil act, that did not originate from some passion or appetite of the body" (Ballou, 34). Evil acts, according to Ballou, arise from lustful desires of the flesh. He further asserted, "[S]in is the natural fruit of the flesh [and] like other fruit is dissolved in dust and can no longer be produced" (Ballou, 35). In short, the source of human sin is not mental but physical. The body's desires, feelings, and affections, Ballou insisted, must be held accountable.

Channing could not hold the body accountable, Ballou now reasoned, without conceding the role of the body in sin. In other words, Channing *had* to separate the mind from the body's own sentiments. If Channing believed that the body is indeed the source of lustful desires, so went Ballou's implicit reasoning, Channing would have been forced to concede Ballou's point that when the body dies, so, too, do the mind's lustful desires. Channing must therefore deny this consequent claim, by denying the antecedent. Instead, Channing must posit the human mind as an entity impervious to embodied sentiment. This is the errant logic Ballou deemed Channing to have used to reach such an irrational, wrongheaded conclusion.

Ballou thus rejected the mind/body split espoused by Channing. Channing's doctrine of human nature, Ballou concluded, was counterfactual and led to a description of a vituperative God that was anathema to Universalist sentiment. Instead, Ballou proffered his own doctrine of human nature, which affirmed the integrity of an embodied humanity. This doctrine let Ballou construct a doctrine of an all-inclusive, merciful God.

Ballou defined human nature as the experience of the integration of the mind and the body as codeterminate faculties. The continuity of human experience, Ballou insisted, entails the active engagement of *both* the mind and the body. Human wholeness is a continuum of mental and physical experiences.

Channing was not persuaded. His response to Ballou and his Universalist movement, as Russell E. Miller notes in *The Larger Hope: The First Century of the Universalist Church in America, 1770–1870*, was "openly hostile." Thus, when "Ballou moved to Boston he was offered no ministerial courtesies or fellowship. It was reported that Channing treated him as though he were a leper" (Miller, 800).

Channing had already accused some who held views similar to Ballou's of "thinking lightly of sin" (Channing, 213). He reminded his readers of Proverbs 14:9 with its claim that "Fools make a mock of sin." Ballou's doctrine was clearly foolish to Channing. But why was it more than this? Why was it moral leprosy? To answer these questions, we have to peer deeper into the theological divide and examine the nontheological foundation of the debate.

Channing affirmed an independent disembodied mind—an autonomous self—as the essence of human nature. Ballou affirmed an interrelational self, one in which the feelings of the human body codetermine the state of the human mind. Channing believed human identity was completely discrete. For Ballou, it was embodied and thus communal because the body cannot exist without environmental support. Accordingly, sin and salvation for Channing were a strictly individual affair, and for Ballou, a more inclusive corporate affair.

Behind Channing's reasoning, Ballou insisted, is the belief that the individual's fate is solely determined by his or her own actions. Human beings are thereby rendered strictly autonomous agents, determined solely by means of their own activities and decisions. Ballou rejected such claims outright. For him, the individual is not an isolated entity but a communal being.

THE WIDER THEOLOGICAL
HISTORY OF OUR DEBATE

The distinct characterizations of human nature articulated by Channing and Ballou have a common theological history. This history begins in 1521, when the father of the German Protestant Reformation, Martin Luther, made his conscience a theological referent for doctrinal adequacy. He announced this new way of assessing church doctrine when he defied both the Pope and the emperor and, at risk of execution for heresy, refused to recant, saying "I am bound by the Scriptures I have quoted and my conscience is taken captive by God's word. I cannot and will not recant anything, for to act against our conscience is neither safe for us, nor open to us. On this I take my stand. I can do no other. God help me. Amen."[2]

Until then, the foundation for theological truth claims had been the Pope, the church councils, and church tradition. "To claim that these standards could be wrong," one historian notes, "was like denying the rules of logic."[3] Luther denied these rules of logic. He overturned these external truth tests for theological claims by making his conscience the internal test for doctrinal certainty. The exterior, objective, human references and resources for belief were now replaced by an interior, personal, subjective experience: Luther's conscience. Luther called his conscience the bride of Christ, the place in human nature where Christ, as bridegroom, resides (Luther, 120).

Luther's Holy Wars followed. By making conscience the first human reference for religious experience and theological certainty, anyone who troubled or challenged Luther's becalmed conscience was thereby—according to Luther—challenging Christ. And the only kind of person who would challenge Christ, Luther reasoned, must be the Antichrist. Thus Judaists, Muslims, and rebellious peasants were, from Luther's perspective, the Antichrist because they troubled his conscience.

He urged German princes and every law-abiding person who could to "smite, slay, and stab, secretly or openly, remembering that nothing can be more poisonous, hurtful, or devilish than a rebel. It is just as when one must kill a mad dog; if you do not strike him, he will strike you, and a whole land with you." Luther's diatribe against the Jews was so vicious and extensive that Hitler used Luther's writing—verbatim—to help justify his extermination of six million Jews.[4]

Luther thus identified an element in human nature, conscience, as the sure human foundation for discerning the truthfulness of theological claims. But he tried to make this aspect of human nature a strictly religious affair. We must look beyond Luther to find the foundational referent for human nature that is our legacy as Unitarian Universalists today. Nevertheless, what Luther, and subsequently John Calvin—who was part of the second generation of Protestant reformers—did for us was to focus theological attention on human nature (the conscience) as the human foundation for discerning the adequacy of doctrinal claims.[5]

Another step was needed to identify the actual, biological foundation in human nature for this theological discernment process. Friedrich Schleiermacher (1768–1834) took the step that established a living nondoctrinal foundation for creedal belief. This German theologian, Reformed minister, and professor, recognized today as the father of modern liberal theology, separated the biology of religious conviction from the doctrinal certainty of rationally affirmed creedal beliefs.

Schleiermacher, at the age of fourteen, had experienced a change of heart as a member of a Moravian pietistic community. Transformed, born again, and renewed, he spent the rest of his life trying to figure out exactly what he had felt. During his search, he set aside the conscience as the human foundation of religious experience. He also rejected the claim that there was something placed in human nature by God that would automatically make a person a Christian, a theist, and a Protestant.

All religious claims, Schleiermacher argued, entail anthropomorphic projections. All religions are culturally determined. No religious claim is the absolute truth. So what is the foundation in human nature for religious experience? It is not a religious belief, Schleiermacher concluded, because all such beliefs are culturally specific and descriptive of personal ideas. Rather, the foundation of religious experience is a feeling, the feeling of being inextricably connected to everything and everyone (Thandeka 1995).

Poetry and the existential language of religious imagination, as my colleague Laurel Hallman reminded us in her 2003 Berry Street lecture, are part of the way in which we describe these foundational feelings. But Schleiermacher was not content with metaphor and religious existential imagination. He wanted a scientific term for this feeling; he used the term *affect* [*Affekt*].[6]

Today, we define *affect* as the "genetically dictated, emotional operating system of the brain" (Panksepp, 3). It is a nonsensate, internal, physical signal system of the human organism that is genetically predetermined to let us cry, laugh, sweat, smile, and change our tone of voice or body gestures to express the impact of other persons and the world upon us.[7] Schleiermacher made this affect signal system of our bodies the first reference for religious experience. He explained the physical foundation of spirituality as a physical fact of human nature. As such, we can call him the father of affective neurotheology.

Schleiermacher made the first reference for religious experience a biological fact of the human organism: a shift in human affect. But shifting affect is not, itself, religious experience. Rather, the shift, Schleiermacher argued, is felt as a physical impulse, sentiment, emotion, or passion that alters the subjective mood of a person such that a new determinate action or thought occurs. Affect, for Schleiermacher, is thus a pulse of life. It is the felt link between the interior and exterior world of human experience, the link between thought and action. This link is the living continuity of human experience. The entire expansive range of this link is all of life itself.

Affect, Schleiermacher argued, is the organic link between the immediate feeling [*Gefühl*] of our own embodied sense of self and our actions [*Tun*] (Schleiermacher 1830, proposition 3.4). Our thoughts and actions are prompted by affective feelings. Our mental activity is sparked and brought into focus by affective sentiments, impulses, feelings, attitudes, dispositions, and emotions.

Something felt within us affectively sparks our mental attention. We notice, for example, a shift in a person's facial features or tone of voice and we feel uneasy. We see a shadow cast by a person trying to hide behind a streetlight and we begin to sweat.

We can have such experiences because we are a mental-physical or, more precisely, a psyche-soma continuum sending and receiving physical signals through movements, sound, facial configurations, and other biological signal systems. The person feels these signal systems internally and expresses them externally in ways that cue others through discernible dispositional patterning principles of the human organism such as the expressive state of joy or sorrow (Demos, 11).

Schleiermacher believed that each such affect-based shift in our own personal sense of well-being is an inducement or motive for our actions and beliefs. The act or thought that follows the shift in affect will be pious, Schleiermacher concluded, only if the way in which the affect is determined is pious (Schleiermacher 1830, proposition 3.4). For example, we may become outraged because of a personal assault against us. If this outrage, however, is mediated by feelings of compassion rather than revenge, we can figure out a way to attend to our injury, prevent further abuse, and address the problematic behavior of the other without engaging in abusive, assaultive reactions.[8] Similarly, if these determinations of our feelings are religiously defined, the result is a *religious* affection.

Thus, the shift of feeling within us brought on by altered states of human affect is not in itself a pious or religious state. Rather, the shift of feeling, Schleiermacher argued, is an act of human nature. Our affective states shift all the time. Our moods change, our dispositions and sentiments shift all the time. These affect-based alterations of our dispositions are not religious in and of themselves. They become religious only when they are defined that way. Not surprisingly, a religious community will share a similar style of affective expression as a ritualized, traditional style of religious practices (Schleiermacher, 1830, proposition 6.2). One religious community will shout, another will dance; one community will clap, another will not clap at all. The foundation for these differences is the biology of faith, the affective engagement of the human organism with its surrounding environment. The expression is determined by the purposes and principles, religious creeds, doctrines, traditions, and practices of a specific religious community.

I call Schleiermacher's articulation of the biological foundation of religious temperaments and actions Affect Theology. Affect Theology affirms the nontheological, nonrational, affective foundation of all religious claims, doctrines, creeds, and dogma. Nothing, Schleiermacher insists, is directly received from the mind of God to the mind of man. All human knowledge is mediated by *human* feeling. Human beings, from this theological perspective, cannot even say that God has a mind without acknowledging the anthropomorphic projection. More pointedly, in Schleiermacher's scheme, to speak of God is to refer to human consciousness of the feeling of being inextricably linked to life itself as a part of life itself and thus absolutely dependent upon life itself.

The first word that comes to mind to refer to this feeling of absolute dependence—for Christians, Schleiermacher argues—is *God* (Schleiermacher, 1830, proposition 4.4; Thandeka 1995, 23–24, 105–110). For Buddhists, the first word might be *Sunyata;* for Pagans, *Gaia;* for Humanists, the infinite, uncreated *Universe.* In sum, *all* religious talk, all religious claims are prompted by and thus have as their first reference human feelings. To ignore these feelings is to project human experience into an abstract realm and then to make it seem as if we are receiving our most sacred truths from on high.[9]

Affect Theology explains how discrete religious traditions all refer to the same biological foundation of human experience: the pulse of life felt as the affective link between self and other, self and world. This affective link constitutes the self's experience of its own integrity as a coherent, congruent, and integrated aspect of the rhythmic pulse of life.[10] Here we find the living foundation of religious belief.

Shifts in human affect are deemed religious because they are described, recounted, explained, and articulated as experiences within a particular religious tradition. But the primary stage of the experience is not religious in and of itself. It is simply a shift in human affect. The first reference for disparate religious traditions and beliefs is the human affective experience of the pulse of life itself, which Schleiermacher called the "natal hour of everything living in religion."[11] This expansion, extension, sustenance, and inclusion of all in all is the breath of life itself [*ruah, spiritus*].

Schleiermacher gave liberal theology a basic vocabulary to affirm the human feelings of religious experience in noncreedal ways, by identifying the nonreligious, biological element in human nature that is foundational for religious experience. He gave us, in short, an Affect Theology, a noncreedal theological vocabulary that identifies the affective human foundation of religious experience as the pulse of life itself.[12] Schleiermacher thus made rationally constructed, cognitive, theological reflections; concepts; claims; propositions; creeds; and doctrines secondary to this living feeling of the expanse of life.

But a funny thing happened to Schleiermacher's Affect Theology when he tried to explain it to his contemporaries in the Introduction to *The Christian Faith*. Schleiermacher's careful attempt to explain why affective states of the self are the foundational reference for Christian doctrine and the content of Christian theology was roundly condemned by his contemporaries as pagan, papist, Gnostic, pantheistic, and self-contradictory (Schleiermacher 1981, 34–36).

Then a new debate began. If the foundation of religion is indeed a human experience that can be explained in scientific terms, this experience surely must be human *reason* rather than human *feeling*. Schleiermacher's biological foundation for faith was thus rejected by the theological tradition—modern liberal theology—that looks back to Schleiermacher as its father.

The next step of our investigation of a noncreedal formulation for the biological foundation of our faith begins here. Here we find Immanuel Kant (1724–1804), who, as one Kantian scholar reminds us, had already rejected pietistic feelings as a sure foundation for faith (Kant 1960, xiii–xiv). The sure human foundation for liberal faith was not feeling, Kant insisted, but reason. More specifically, the foundation was duty dictated by the universal laws of reason (Kant 1993, 129). Moral duty, Kant argued, applied to every activity of one's own life.

Schleiermacher wanted to give balance to this rationalist approach by emphasizing affect as the complement to Kant's theology. Schleiermacher succeeded in identifying affect as the biological source of the theological complement to rational theology. But he did not succeed in making this referent the biological foundation for the liberal tradition to which his work gave birth.

Rather, the shift in focus from affect and reason (Schleiermacher) to reason only (Kant) in the liberal religious traditions that dominate our theological landscape today is epitomized in the oft-repeated summary of this liberal tradition celebrated by Earl Morse Wilbur in the introduction to *A History of Unitarianism: Socinianism and Its Antecedents*:

> It is intended here ... to present not so much the history of a particular sect or form of Christian *doctrine,* as to consider broadly the development of a movement fundamentally characterized instead by its steadfastness and increasing devotion to these three leading *principles*: first, complete mental freedom in religion rather than bondage to creeds or confessions; second, the unrestricted use of reason in religion, rather than reliance upon external authority or past tradition; third, generous tolerance of differing religious views and usages rather than insistence upon uniformity in doctrine, worship, or polity. Freedom, reason, and tolerance: it is these conditions above all others that this movement has from the beginning increasingly sought to promote ... (Wilbur, 5).

Wilbur highlights the rational space needed to let liberal religion flourish. But reason is not enough. As Unitarian Universalist minister, theologian, church institutionalist, and first vice president of the Unitarian Universalist Association Raymond C. Hopkins notes in his groundbreaking *A Functional Philosophy for the Liberal Church*:

> Mere intellectualism and correct theology will not result in worship or in concrete religious action. No mere intellectual philosophy of life is enough no matter how true it is. Our religious conclusions must be given emotional support or they will never serve our people.

Nevertheless, Hopkins, like Wilbur, makes rational theology the foundational principle of our liberal tradition. For Hopkins, "the heart of religion lies . . . in man's response to religious ideas."[13]

And thus we arrive at our dominant theological situation today: We have been looking inside our minds for the right foundational *idea* for liberal religion because we profess that the sure foundation of our liberal faith is "the free use of reason."[14] And thus our predicament is that we cannot conceive of a common rational foundation for our religious movement that would not, by definition, be a creed, propositional claim, or idea, and thus a contradiction to our own self-professed stance as a noncreedal people. Accordingly, the resolution to our search for a foundational human experience becomes impossible. The search can never be completed because the solution usually proposed is self-contradictory.

Thus begins the pervasive, theological conundrum of liberal theology. When liberal religionists and theorists make reason and ideas a human foundation of religious faith, critique becomes the primary way this faith is explained. Paul Tillich called it the Protestant Principle.[15]

In his book *Erring: A Postmodern A/theology*, Mark C. Taylor gives the classic contemporary presentation of this self-critical stance of liberal religion. Taylor's work displays the remains of the liberal theologian who now realizes that his tradition has turned him into a wanderer. This wanderer is deeply unsettled, an "undomesticated drifter, always suspicious of stopping, staying, and dwelling. . . . Attached to no home and *always* separated from father and mother, the wanderer is nameless. What appeared to be a proper name always turns out to be an improper mark. Homeless and anonymous, the wanderer 'doesn't even know who he is,' doesn't even know his identity—for *he has no identity*" (Taylor, 156–577).

Taylor's wandering theologian is someone whose liberal religious tradition lacks a coherent biological foundational, an internal, felt sense of agency with others and the natural world. So reason goes it alone searching for nothing in particular.

When Affect Theology retrieves and reaffirms the biological foundation of liberal theology as the living foundation of rational theology, these theological ramblings will end. Affect Theology thus acknowledges the cogency of James Luther Adams's critique of rational theology with its one-sided reliance on the ancient Greek "intellectualistic or rationalistic view [of reason as the master principle of creation]." Adams writes:

> What is to be especially noted here is the tendency of this intellectualistic view, first to interpret existence in terms of a rational, unified, harmonious structure, and, second to exalt the cognitive, nonaffective aspects of the human psyche."[16]

This rationalist view, as Adams rightly argues, has been an "increasingly dominant force in modern Western culture." Adams advocates, in contrast, voluntarism (the activities of the "individual through association"[17]), which "although for the most part [insists] upon the basic significance of the intellectual disciplines, has tended to stress the dynamic and contradictory elements in existence and the affective aspects of human nature."[18]

Like James Luther Adams, our Affect Theology will emphasize the "affective aspects of human nature." We also advance Adams's claims because we can make use of contemporary scientific insights. The results will give us a systematic Unitarian Universalist theology for the twenty-first century.

It seems fair to say that, collectively, Unitarian Universalists proffer more theologies than any other single group of religious people in the world. We espouse, to name only a few, theistic, agnostic, atheistic, Christian, Judaic, Pagan, Humanist, Eco-Feminist, Earth Centered, Buddhist, and Hindu Unitarian

Universalist theologies. Moreover, we celebrate this diversity of *personal* belief as proof of our *institutional* noncreedal foundation.

This affirmation of our theological diversity, however, does not disclose the source of our collective unity as one religious people. Quite the contrary. This diversity poses a problem for us theologically, when we attempt to discern the source of our unity by looking for the unifying idea or other rational claims. As we have seen, our rational theological approaches simply sunder us anew because the ground of our unity as one religious people is not an *idea*.

Our foundation is an actual *living* fact of our lives, which is felt affectively and then displayed rationally through articulation of these affective personal experiences. Presently, we do not affirm this common biological foundation of our beliefs because we can't. Our theological methods for discerning it—our doctrine of human nature—are conflicted. Nevertheless, we experience it.

One way in which we experience this noncreedal biological foundation of our religious tradition *before* it is conceptualized theistically or nontheistically will clarify my point. It will also help us understand why we need Affect Theology.

The setting is Prague, capital of the Czech Republic. The date is Wednesday, May 28, 2003. It is the beginning of my workshop on small group ministries (covenant groups), for the delegates, staff, and visitors attending the annual meeting of the International Council of Unitarians and Universalists.

As the group of about sixty people settles into the chairs carefully arranged in a circle at the back of the council's small meeting room, I think about what I learned earlier in the day when I listened to the delegates' reports. I learned that Unitarianism is registered by the German government as a philosophical society. In Spain, the status of Unitarians as a religious or secular group has not yet been decided by the government. The Danish Unitarians do not introduce their young people to their religion or offer them any religious education programs until they are teenagers to avoid restricting freedom of thought. I learned that the average size of a Unitarian congregation in England is twenty members. I also learned that some of the people present at this conference were

Christians; others were Humanists. At least one self-identified Unitarian believed that not only is Jesus God, but also that Jesus died to save a sinful humanity, was resurrected on the third day, and now is seated at the right hand of God.

The group finally settled down. Someone lit the chalice on a small table in the center of our circle, as I read the liturgical words of Christine Robinson, #448 in the UUA hymnal, *Singing the Living Tradition*:

> *We gather this hour as people of faith*
> *With joys and sorrows, gifts and needs,*
> *We light this beacon of hope, sign of our quest*
> *For truth and meaning,*
> *In celebration of the life we share together.*

After a few introductory remarks, I asked the participants to sit comfortably in their chairs. I continued, "Lower your eyes and simply listen to the sounds in the room." Two minutes later, I said, "Now listen to the sound of your own heart beating." Another two minutes ticked by and then I said, "Listen to the sounds in the room again." After another minute, I brought this first set of exercises to a close and said, "If any of you noticed a difference between the first and second times you listened to the sounds in the room, tell us what you discovered. Describe what you experienced." We then listened as some astonished participants described how they'd heard their heartbeat or the heartbeats of others in the room. Some participants described the comforting feeling of stillness they felt as they sank into and became part of the sounds in the room. Some noted how much more relaxed they felt. One said he had fallen asleep. Some said they had not discerned a difference in the room the second time they listened.

In the next exercise, I asked participants to take out a pencil or pen. We then stared at our respective pens and pencils for three minutes. Other exercises followed that also began and ended with focused attention on a sensate experience. After each series of exercises, I asked the participants to describe their experience. By the end of the workshop, one woman said she had felt God. Another said he had seen a spirit moving around the room. Several said they'd discovered something about their religion, a feeling of repose they had not known existed, which made them feel a new depth of trust and love for the people around them. One man said he always hoped for a miraculous moment at these conferences and this workshop, for him, had provided that moment. Many described a heightened awareness accompanied by a deep and abiding sense of peace, relaxation, and cessation of inner turmoil. All were amazed by the variety and diversity of ideas used to express the simple set of experiences they had shared together. By the end of the two-hour series of these "embodied practices" and thoughtful reflections, everyone present, in one way or another, noted the profound sense of trust and ease that enveloped the group and filled the room.

Each set of experiences began with the invitation to become aware of something through sensation (seeing, listening, touching). Each set of experiences ended with the invitation to reflect, rationally, upon what was felt. The rational reflections produced a diverse series of cognitive claims (theistic and nontheistic). The experiences these claims presupposed, however, were not abstract ideas, but the sensations of bodies awash in the affective sentiments produced by the physical stirrings of the world within them and around them. The first awareness of these stirrings is the foundation of our engagement with the world. These stirrings refer to the biology of our beliefs, our human capacity to be transformed and renewed by feeling. Our Unitarian Universalist doctrine of human nature must refer us back to this foundation of our faith and explain the biological processes entailed in this experience.

A CONTEMPORARY SCIENTIFIC VOCABULARY FOR AFFECT THEOLOGY

Affect Theology is a doctrine of human nature. Its basic claim is that humans are relational beings who cue each other interaffectively. This capacity for interaffective attunement is a defining aspect of human character; the basic building block of human community; the biological reference for religious experience; and the felt, living content of rational theological claims.

Contemporary affective neuroscience and affect theory help us understand the nature and structure of this interaffective human experience. The groundbreaking work of developmental psychologist Daniel N. Stern gives us a way into this contemporary work through his analysis of the "vitality affects" of human nature. In *The Interpersonal World of the Infant*, Stern begins with an analysis of how mental acts, which he defines as "perception, feeling, cognition, remembering," are linked to the human body. According to Stern, all mental acts

> are accompanied by input from the body, including, importantly, internal sensations. This input includes the momentary states of arousal, activation, tonicity, levels of motivational activation or satiety (in various systems), and well-being.... The other input from the body includes all the things the body does or must do to permit, support, amplify (etc.) the ongoing mental activity (perceiving, thinking, etc.), such as postures formed or held, movements (of the eyes, head, or body), displacement in space, and contractions and relaxations of muscular tone. The body is never doing nothing.... All these body signals come from the self—an as-yet-unspecified self. Such signals need not be attended to. They need not enter into awareness. Yet they are there in the background. They are the continuous music of being alive. That is why I refer to changes or modulations in this music as vitality affects.... It is this music that will permit the emergent self...to appear. But first it must be yoked with a mental activity.[19]

These "internal sensations" are our interior sense of being alive. When we pay attention to our physical state, we are internally aware of small impulses, rhythmic movements, temperatures, dryness and moisture, stimulations, and so much more, which physically codify a lived moment of our lives as human organisms.

These "vitality affects," also referred to as "background feelings,"[20] are always with us because they are our sense of being alive. We do not merely *feel* these affects. As organic beings, we *are* these affects.

Neurologist Antonio Damasio notes that these affective states give our lives and thoughts definition and color.[21] They are our body language and are observable as "body postures, the shape and design of our movements, and even the tone of our voices and the prosody in our speech as we communicate thoughts that may have little to do with the background emotions."[22]

This coloring, as Damasio points out, is not the same as our foreground emotions such as fear, sorrow, joy, or anger. This is why he calls them our "background feelings." These feelings are the tonality of our lives, the pervasive dispositions of our being, the way in which we feel everything because we saturate what we know with what we feel. When this vast field of our being is matched affectively with the vast affective field of another person and with all of life, we feel attuned to life itself. This affective attunement is the "natal hour of everything living in religion" (Schleiermacher). This state is not an idea of the self but a state of the self. It is a living moment, interaffectively felt. It is life.

Stern suggests that interaffectivity "may be the first, most pervasive, and most immediately important form of sharing subjective experiences." Abstract concepts and disembodied ideas are not the medium for identifying and experiencing similar feeling states.[23] The bond is affective, interactive, and embodied. Human beings achieve this matching of subjective feelings in the self and other by using physical cues such as facial expressions. The self that emerges within this organic system of communication is a self-in-intimate-relationship-with-an-other. This self is a continuum of affective engagement linked to ideas patterned after, generated by, and symbolized as these formative interaffective experiences.

Affect neurobiologist and psychoanalytic theorist Allan N. Schore summarizes this point with precision. "Human development," Schore argues, "including its internal neurochemical and neurobiological mechanisms, cannot be understood apart from this affect-transacting relationship."[24]

As human organisms with brains that coordinate affect signal systems, our genetic programming makes us capable of empathizing with others because we physically recognize (match) facial expressions, physical gestures, and tones of voice as part of our own physical vocabulary for altered feelings. We share a genetically coded physical language of human sentiment and desire. These shared neurobiological facts of our species make it possible for us, as affect theorist Virginia Demos notes, to read each other's body intonations, gestures, and facial expressions to make inferences about what triggered the expression, what affective experience is produced, and what the response to this experience will be (Demos, 11).

Jaak Panksepp, one of the leaders in contemporary affective neuroscience, pays close attention to the nature and structure of these affective signal systems. Panksepp believes we are now on the verge of an "affective revolution," which will force the academic community to redefine the way in which it thinks about human nature. The "evidence for basic brain substrates for [basic] emotions is massive," Panksepp argues, "and those who choose to disagree with their existence have probably not read a sufficient amount of the available neurobehavioral literature" (Panksepp, 348–352).

These affective neurobehavioral and neurobiological processes of the human organism, Panksepp argues, are not the same as the cultural perspectives and ciphers used to describe and alter them. Panksepp thus investigates the ways in which triggered affective experiences emerge from the biochemical, electrical, molecular, and neurological systems in the brain that constitute the organizing centers of emotions. Affective neuroscience requires a detailed analysis of the biological basis for emotions such as fear, anger, sorrow, and joy in humans and other mammals. Panksepp's work gives us the precision of medical science when describing the foundation of the nonverbal living communication system of human beings.

The first premise of Affect Theology, as a doctrine of human nature, is that human experience is not a solo act. It is interaffective. The human soul *is* an interaffective expanse of engagement; it is the human experience of a continuity of being as a continuum of relationships that expand and enhance the spiritual well-being of all. This spiritual well-being is our breath of life, our experience of life itself, inspiring us affectively as the feeling of absolute interdependence with all. As such, the soul of our religious community (and the spirit of each of its members) is an expanse of our affective engagements as life-enhancing rather than life-diminishing experiences.

Affect theorist Virginia Demos's description of successful communication with infants provides an illustration of this first premise of Affect Theology. Demos calls these human communication signals the "cues."[25]

> These cues—a combination of facial expressions, vocalizations, and body movements—convey information primarily about the infant's affective state and the infant's plans and goals in relation to that state. Indeed, before the advent of language and other symbolic forms of representation, the infant's affective expressive behaviors are probably the only reliable and valid indication of the saliency of events for the infant; they thereby constitute the primary medium of communication and meaning in the infant-mother system (Demos, 11).

This affect-based system of communication between infant and caretaker goes in two directions because both infant and caretaker must make inferences based on affective expressions.

A baby's survival depends upon its ability to send and receive these physical signals through movements, sounds, facial configurations, and other discrete sets of neurochemical, biological signals that can be read by others. Without this physical signal system, the baby's caretaker cannot know, for example, when the infant is hungry.

Failure of a caretaker to attend to this affective foundation of human communication can blunt the infant's newly emerging sense of self and sunder the child's psychological sense of wholeness.

This negative fact of our interaffective, interdependent nature is the basis of Affect Theology's second premise: human emotional breakdown is not a solo act. It, too, is interaffective. If we cannot alter our environment through affective engagement, attunement, and interaffective interchange, our affective system breaks down as the unifying source of our sense of life. The vitality aspects of human life are blunted.

The psychoanalytic work of D. W. Winnicott gives us an initial set of images for this more troubling aspect of our "background feelings" of being alive. He describes what can happen to an emerging sense of self when caretakers repeatedly miss, ignore, or deny a child's genetically predetermined attempts as a newly emerging self to communicate affectively. These newly forming selves can split.

To make this point, Winnicott, a pediatrician and child psychiatrist, begins with a basic observation: the human experience of continuity is not innate but "achieved" (Winnicott 1989, 566). In short, "There's no such thing as a baby" (Winnicott 1992, 99). There must be a caretaker if there is to be a baby. If there is no caretaker, then there is no baby. This psyche-soma continuum is the baby's interactive living foundation for an emerging sense of self.

Winnicott notes that if the environment is not sufficient to support the drive toward continuity of being of the newborn, and not "good enough" to support and sustain the actual experiences of a continuity of being of the infant and then the child, the developmental continuum breaks up, which puts the child's continuity of being as a psychologically integrated self at risk.

When this continuum breaks up, "the basis for a psychosomatic split is laid down" (Winnicott 1989, 566). The source of this split is the breakup of the caretaking environment as a sustaining and life-enhancing holding and handling facility for the child (Winnicott 1989, 567). This breakup of the caretaking environment can in turn produce within the child an "overactivity of the mental functioning."

A disembodied mind is born of this "overactivity of the mental functioning," a mind that acts as if it alone is needed to sustain the self. This newly constructed self-defined independent mind, Winnicott argues, eventually begins to "take over and organize the caring for the psyche-soma" (Winnicott, 1992, 246).

According to Winnicott, "In health, the mind does not usurp the environment's function, but makes possible an understanding and eventually a making use of its relative failure" (Winnicott 1992, 246). But in an unsupportive environment, the mind begins to act as if it is the environment for the psyche-soma, and "the psyche of the individual gets 'seduced' away into this mind from the intimate relationship which the psyche originally had with the soma" (Winnicott, 1992, 246–247).

Winnicott rightly concludes that the belief that the mind is independent of the body can be traced back to this breakdown of the continuity between psyche and soma, mind and body. Winnicott calls this breakdown the origin of the so-called mind-body problem in Western philosophy (Winnicott 1992, 243). The source of this breakdown is the toxic nature of the environment in which the child is forced to live. Human environments become environmental hazards first for the child and then for the adult. The environments destroy the persons they produce.

The result of this breakdown is "a mind-psyche, which is pathological" (Winnicott 1992, 247). Affect is displayed and then hidden (Winnicott 1992, 100, 180). The self wages war with itself, mind against feelings, heart against head, reason against passion. The affective space between self and other, which Winnicott calls the "intermediate area of experience" (Winnicott 1971, 13–14), is ruptured. The cognitive link or mental "yoke" (Daniel N. Stern) between self and other is broken. One mind of this ruptured self is a disembodied rationality; the other is filled with aggrieved affections.

This breakdown of the psyche-soma continuum can split the self. This split self, argues psychologist Arnold Goldberg in his groundbreaking *Being of Two Minds: The Vertical Split in Psychoanalysis and Psychotherapy,* is a person who *knowingly* takes up residence in two distinct and contradictory psychological worlds. Such people live as if they are two: they binge and then feel shame; they steal even though they could buy the item and then are demoralized by their action; they are grandiose and then feel diminished by their outrageous behavior; they lie and then feel morally demeaned by their deceit.

All of us sometimes act against our highest moral values. But when such actions reduce us to an internal battlefield that cannot be resolved, we have ventured into the terrain of a split self. We must now find the vocabulary needed to explain the collusion principle entailed in splitting the self.

Persons with split selves, according to Goldberg, are conscious of the other part of themselves; repressed selves are not. Split selves are aware of an alternative structure within themselves. The separation is thus vertical rather than horizontal. The "split self" thus refers to a "side-by-side" (i.e., vertical) existence of disparate personalities within the self that despise the values and actions of each other. According to Goldberg, the psyche of such persons thus seems to move back and forth between multiple realities. As long as this failure of reconciliation endures, there will be a heavy emotional price (Goldberg, 9). Unlike the "horizontal line called the repression barrier" (Goldberg, 10), which prevents conscious awareness of the repressed self, the vertical line does not stave off awareness of an alternative self structure.

Split selves cannot be achieved alone. The vertical split in a person's psychic life derives from parental collusion. Parent and child, Goldberg argues, construct the split self together by separating affective experiences that must be attended to, *are* attended to, and then result in punishment for being attended to. In other words, the parent gives the child tacit permission for doing something that is deeply pleasurable and then punishes the child for having done it.

The emotional principle behind splitting is thus one of both pain and pleasure (Goldberg, 73). It is pleasurable because the affective experience triggers a bodily experience of satiation that is deeply gratifying. It is punishing because the affective experience is identified as bad and wrong. Persons in this conflicted environment must have the affective experience for the sake of their overall bodily integrity and then must condemn the experience for the sake of their learned social values. Writes Goldberg: "The parental directions given to the child, both explicitly and implicitly, demanded a division into these side-by-side sectors" (Goldberg, 9). This is the collusion principle: parent and child together split the child's self, and then both parent and child reward and punish the child for this splitting (Goldberg, 43–58).

Goldberg does not blame the parent for wrongdoing; rather he explains how both the child and the parent operate as split selves. He explains human behavior psychoanalytically as an interaffective field of human engagement and disengagement. His point is that collusion functions in the lives of *both* child and parent to address a structural gap in the parental caregiving affective system of the child. The child (with the parent's assistance), constructs a self-care affective system, in response to a gap in its caretaking system. This constructed self with its discrete, affect-based, emotional world of rules and values, allows the child to handle the structural deficits in its relationship to the parent. This "misbehaving" avoids a far more difficult and painful state, which the reintegration of the child's emotional life would reveal (Goldberg, 27). Revealed would be absence of an interaffectively nurturing and life enhancing, caretaking environment for the child. Goldberg concludes that a "failure of synthesis [thus] characterizes this pathology." The child becomes, in effect, a being of two minds. The price for retaining this split "both saps the energy that would be available to an integrated person and demands an accounting for living in a real world" (Goldberg, 27).

Rather than experience the loss and disappointment of parental failure, the child engages in an affect-saturated action that is both pleasurable (e.g., bingeing) and punishing (e.g., feelings of guilt and shame). The psychological developmental principle becomes one of disavowal (Goldberg, 43). This twofold affective structure functions as a substitute self-structure, one that replicates without addressing the real source of the problem.

Together parent and child set up a scheme of interaffectivity in which the child relates to itself as if it is two beings (two minds) instead of one. The child creates an "other" for itself—a second mind—a substitute for the longed-for life-sustaining affections of its caretaker.

The collusion of the caretakers in this scheme is hidden from view by the child's own self-pleasing, self-blaming schemes. Solutions to this problem can very easily focus only on the activity of the child and the adult he or she becomes.

It is here that we discover the difference between contemporary affect theory and Affect Theology. Psychoanalytic affect theorists explain the pathology and endeavor to heal the individual. Affect Theology acknowledges the pathology and endeavors to heal the individual and the community through liturgical practices and social justice work.

A VOCABULARY FOR AFFECT THEOLOGY

Affect Theology uses the religious language of sin and salvation to explain how this healing work is accomplished as a religious practice. We must redefine these two terms, *sin* and *salvation*. If we simply discard the terms, we lose access to the debates, insights, judgments, and reflections that inform our religious history as Unitarian Universalists. We have a religious genealogy. Religious genealogy, to be sure, is not destiny. It is, however, directive. The direction of Unitarian Universalism today is greatly informed by our past. This past is conflicted. We need a new language of reverence to sort out these conflicts and resolve them. Each resolution advances us as a coherent, engaged, and reenlivened religious people. We update ourselves and in so doing transform ourselves.

Accordingly, Affect Theology uses the term *sin* to refer to the breakdown of the human interaffective system of communication. The facilitating environments (the extended caretaking system of home, work, church, nation, and world community) disrupt rather than enhance the natural neurobiological predisposition to communicate interaffectively and expansively to ensure a sense of well-being, coherence, congruence, and body integrity.[26] Sin keeps people and communities from healing and transforming the world. Sin destroys the human experience of salvation by sundering the self, the community, and the world.

Sin is the disembodiment of the self, which produces an inability to remain in community openheartedly. Sin is this broken state of the self and the world. The splitting off of human affections from ideas, thoughts, and actions is explosive.[27] The wrenched affections return in the form of affective rage, despair, disruption, and shame. Genocide and racism, sexism, and classism—the sins of humanity against itself—are born of massive collective eruptions of discordant human affections.

The term *salvation* refers to the human experience of a sustained, expansive interaffective system of communication that enables the person to (1) sustain herself or himself through empathic engagement with others, (2) be aware of the feelings of self and others as a space of creative affective engagement and interchange that can be negotiated to enhance and ensure personal and collective well-being for all, and (3) create a communication system that articulates and advances a social justice agenda for all.

Human salvation is thus a corporate affair. We were not conceived, born, or individuated alone. If others did not exist (including the wider world of nature and the universe) we would not be here. We could not be here. A basic eco-biological law of nature is that organisms cannot flourish without an environment that nurtures, sustains, and enhances their developmental continuity through life-affirming relationships. Our human affections are thus deeply private and utterly social. We feel the world upon us and within us. The world stirs our affections. We are a pulse of its life.

Our very nature as interaffective organisms means that the touch of another becomes the matter of engagement first felt. Each body-based feeling is a new creation of the world and an expression of the primal fact of human life: interaffective engagement. The rituals and traditions established to celebrate, protect, and enhance interaffective engagement define a religious way of life, the way in which persons connect themselves to one another for spiritual uplift, moral agency, and liberative social action (Thandeka 2002, 20).

Affect Theology, using its definitions of sin and salvation, affirms, in contemporary terms, our Universalist doctrine of universal salvation, which proclaims human beings are interaffective selves and thus are capable of reintegrative, salvific experiences of a continuity of being. We can be born "not once or twice but again and again forever" (Owen-Towle, 10) because the living foundation of human life is life itself. The embracing repose of life itself restores us. It inspires us anew.

Psychoanalytic theorist Judith Lewis Herman affirms the restorative, renewing, and salvific agency of this living foundation of human life in her work with severely traumatized abused persons, whom she calls survivors. She describes one of the processes of their recovery:

> Repeatedly in the testimony of survivors there comes a moment when a sense of connection is restored by another person's unaffected display of generosity. Something in herself that the victim believes to be irretrievably destroyed—faith, decency, courage—is reawakened by an example of common altruism. Mirrored in the actions of others, the survivor recognizes and reclaims a lost part of herself. At that moment, the survivor begins to rejoin the human commonality.[28]

This restorative process begins, Herman observes, "with the discovery that one is not alone." Affect Theology describes this sense of affective mirroring, this matching of human feelings, this restorative process of human engagement, as the vitality principle of our lives. It is the living foundation of our Unitarian Universalist doctrine of human nature. We are enlivened anew because we are relational beings.

Our doctrine of universal salvation also explains the power of the small group ministry movement transforming so many of our congregations. Small group ministries (also called covenant groups) create and thereby are liturgical practices. Members of the group experience the ongoing, life-sustaining, and enhancing salvific continuity of openhearted and open-minded engagement as the living ground of faith. Affect Theology affirms this movement in Unitarian Universalism as a major expression of our contemporary doctrine of universal salvation today.

These small groups of six to twelve people meet twice a month in each other's homes. They also do communal social justice work together. Feelings are noted, disappointments acknowledged, hopes expressed, and joys celebrated. (See www.the-ccv.org for details.) Covenant groups thus remind their members — through the sacramental practice of creative interaffective engagement—that the human body is a sacred ground of right relationship. This experience of life-affirming engagement can enhance the soul of our religious association. Feelings that sustain and support our well-being individually and collectively re-create us again and again.

Affect Theology's doctrine of human nature derives two approaches from its premises, definitions, and embodied practices: (1) when in the presence of persons who believe they are disembodied minds, look for unacknowledged affect, (2) act with compassionate understanding toward persons who espouse theologies of a disembodied mind. These two approaches allow us to resolve the debate between Channing and Ballou by finding and affirming the foundational unity and coherence of human engagement upon which their disputed claims rest.

THE DEBATE BETWEEN CHANNING AND BALLOU RESOLVED

Affect Theology proffers two initial hypotheses about Channing's doctrine of human nature. First, both Channing's doctrine and his theology of sin and salvation might have been significantly shaped by his own childhood experience of trying to survive "stoically" (Mendelsohn 1971) in affectively arid and financially trying times. Second, Channing's doctrine might be the product of someone who replicates, theologically, his own experience of giving his mind an independent status and allowing it to function in isolation, in lieu of a nonsustaining, ill-nurturing environment. Channing despised his own body's affections, as we learn from the first volume of his biography, which includes some of his memoirs, edited by his nephew William Henry Channing.

Beginning at age nineteen, Channing worked for two years as tutor for the children of a wealthy Virginia family. He lived apart from the family and set up a physical routine that compromised his health. He usually worked at his desk until two or three o'clock in the morning. Frequently, the sun would rise before he went to bed. When he did go to sleep, he often used the bare floor as his bed. This was his way of trying to overcome what he thought of as his effeminacy, as his nephew tells us. Once on the floor, he would spring up at any hour and walk about in the cold in an attempt to toughen his heart. Channing also experimented with his diet and did not exercise. As a result of these routines, he broke down his immune system and was infirm for the rest of his life (Channing 1848, 96–97).

During this period of his life, Channing was also depressed. He saw slavery firsthand and hated it, but he remained silent. He despised his task of visiting the slaves' huts and distributing their weekly rations. Once, when the master and mistress were away, Channing was left "in the entire charge of these beings made hapless by constraint and dependence" (Channing 1848, 84). His "pleasing social relations with the slaveholders," Channing's nephew tells us, "did not deaden his conscience" (Channing 1848, 83).

Channing describes what was going on inside him: "Language cannot express my detestation of it. Master and slave!" (Channing 1848, 85). Channing thus silenced the sentiments of his own heartfelt affections, the life pulse of his being. This silence made him an isolate within his own environment and a jailer of his own affective feelings. He was his own jailer, a prisoner in his own life.

We also discover from his memoirs that this profound sense of affective isolation from his own feelings had happened to him before. His father, an eminent Rhode Island attorney, had died when Channing was thirteen. Channing said that he remembered his father with fondness. Nevertheless, he noted that his father "was a strict disciplinarian at home, and, according to the mistaken notions of that time, kept me at too great a distance from him" (Channing 1848, 16). His father had little time for the family (Channing 1848, 15). Channing, who was sent away to prepare for college, hardly saw his father after reaching the age of twelve (Channing 1848, 21).

Channing's mother lived until Channing was in his fifties, and they both considered their relationship a blessing (Channing 1848, 21). Nevertheless, we learn from Channing that his mother's love was qualified. It "was without illusion. She recognized unerringly and with delight fairness, honesty, genuine uprightness, and shrunk as by instinct from everything specious, the factitious in character, and plausible manners" (Channing 1848, 20). She could be "chillingly severe," Jack Mendelsohn tells us in his biography of Channing (Mendelsohn, 19).

Channing did not seem to fare well, interaffectively, in this household, which, after his father's death was financially impoverished and cast a "shade of premature seriousness [on] his character" (Channing 1848, 42). We learn that as a boy, Channing was

> for the most part grave and reflective. He was fond of lonely rambles on the beach; liked to go apart into some beautiful scene, with no other playmate than his kite, which he delighted in flying; indulged in revery [sic] and contemplation, and according to his own statement, owed the tone of his character more to the influences of solitary thought than of companionship. Indeed, he often said that he understood happiness of childhood rather from observation than experience, that his early life was sad, that conscious want of virtue and knowledge then depressed him, that friendship seemed tame and cold, that life looked desolate, and that every year had been brighter to him than the last (Channing 1848, 35–36).

Channing's reflections as a new minister reveal his lifelong dissatisfaction with positive, affective feelings. The "surest" faith for Channing cannot be a "faith of happiness." He explains why in an autobiographical reflection, noting that his faith

> grew up under a dark sky, and the light has been increasing to this day. My passion for happiness spent itself in my youth in reverie. I never thought of realizing the vision on earth, and yet it has, in a humble manner, been realized. My faith in God, schooled by trial, looked to him first and almost exclusively for virtue, for deliverance from the great evil of sin, which I early felt to be the only true evil. The consciousness of unworthiness repressed all hopes of immediate happiness, gave me a profound conviction of the *justice* of my suffering, turned all my reproaches from Providence on myself, and not only made me incapable of murmuring, but taught me gratitude for the discipline of life. How often, in disappointment, has my first utterance been thanks to the Purifier of the soul!
>
> Thus my faith has never for a moment been shaken by suffering. The consciousness of unworthiness, of falling so far below my idea of duty, a feeling which hardly forsakes me, has helped much to reconcile me to outward evil. It has taken the sting from human reproach. In listening to the inward reprover I have cared little for human opinion, and have found too much truth in censure to be much displeased with any but myself. Accordingly, my religion has taken very much one form; I think of God as Father, from whose power and love I may seek and hope for myself and others the unutterable good—that deliverance from all inward evil, of perfect, unspotted goodness, of spiritual life now and forever.... Happiness has come to me almost as a surprise (Channing 1848, 181–182).

Channing thus seemed to be the perfect minister for his Federal Street Church congregation of Boston Brahmins. As Mendelsohn points out, "Channing knew only too well that what attracted so many of the genteel and fashionable to the pews was the conviction that religion was a powerful means of repressing the vices and passions of the multitude. It was the duty of the best people, therefore, to encourage religion, and to enjoy it—in its more palatable form. And not only to enjoy it, but to spend Sunday afternoons discussing it" (Mendelsohn, 249).

Channing had learned not to speak "out of season," and had been rewarded socially for his silence, as Mendelsohn points out. Moreover, as one German nobleman in his own personal observations of Channing noted, "Channing bleeds for the slaves. Why is he so strangely silent about the condition of free blacks amongst ourselves?" (Mendelsohn, 249, citing Grund, 2: 132–150).

But Channing began to break the rules. He began to speak from his heart, which made him the target of "confusion and contempt." He began to let go, Mendelsohn says, of the "degree of hardness and severity" required to keep the feelings of the human heart in check (Mendelsohn, 249).

The final freeing release came when Channing delivered a eulogy in his church for one of his dearest friends, the abolitionist Charles Follen. The Massachusetts Antislavery Society had requested the use of Channing's church for the service, but the church's standing committee refused. Channing, in defiance of the committee's final decision, delivered a memorial eulogy from the pulpit and then withdrew from the church, leaving behind a ministry of forty years. He left rather than watch his ministry simply peter out in a hostile environment (Mendelsohn, 246–247). His church, like the class of Boston Brahmins it served, was theologically liberal but politically conservative.[29] The topic was slavery, but the personal issue seemed to be feeling.

Thus we might speculate that there is consonance between Channing's doctrine of human nature of the disembodied mind (upon which his doctrine of sin and salvation rests) and his own personal experiences of affective distance from and early disdain for his own embodied feeling. The evidence suggests that Channing conceived of human nature as essentially disembodied and that he separated himself from his feelings to survive in emotionally toxic and socially exploitive communities.

When we review the life of Hosea Ballou, we find a completely different affective scenario. Ballou, the youngest of eleven children, could not recollect his mother because she died when he was two. His father's affection, however, was sustaining, warm, and "uniformly kind and solicitous."[30] We might hypothesize that Ballou learned to affirm the language of his heart's affections because the language of his heart was repeatedly affirmed and sustained by his own home context.

Ballou could have learned through these interaffective, expansive experiences to affirm the integrity of both his head and his heart, to link them as the codeterminate unity foundational to the human experience of wholeness. Human nature, for Ballou, would then mean a mind and body linked as a continuum of life-affirming experiences. This mutual integrity of head and heart would require and deserve articulation as congruency between his well-formed ideas, concepts, and claims and his heartfelt affections. Such a man as Ballou would thus refuse to abandon his heart by disembodying his mind. As his son notes:

> In [Ballou's] researches and reading concerning the creed that he now publicly professed, he found it impossible to bring his heart to conform to the doctrine of eternal reprobation, and this in itself, as he afterwards remarked, was an evidence of no considerable importance, to his mind, that it could not be true; for why should his Heavenly Father have implanted in his heart an earnest desire for the salvation of all mankind, unless that desire was susceptible of gratification, as is every appetite, mental or physical, with which we are endowed by nature? . . . After all this anxious solicitude, this solitary mental struggle, this prayerful communication with Heaven, he at length declared himself a believer in the *final* salvation of the whole human family.[31]

Ballou chose to separate himself from untenable religious doctrines rather than deny his own heartfelt affections. As we also discover, he insisted upon an internal integrity between his mind and heart, his ideas and affective sentiments. Writes Ballou:

I found, when conversing upon the subject [of God's impar-
tial grace], that my Calvinistic tenets could be made either to
result in universal salvation, or to compel me to acknowledge
the partiality of the divine favor. This gave me no small inqui-
etude of mind, as I was unable to derive satisfaction from sentiments which I could not defend. That which more than anything else contributed to turn my thoughts seriously towards
the belief of Universalism, was the ardent desire with which I
found myself exercised that sinners might be brought to
repentance and salvation. I found it utterly impossible to
bring my feelings to consent to the doctrine of eternal repro-
bation, and I was compelled either to allow that such feelings
were sinful, or that my Heavenly Father, in giving them to me,
had implanted an evidence in favor of the salvation of all
men, the force of which I found no means to resist.[32]

Ballou, we might say, refused to sunder himself into a mind at war
with the affective feelings of its body.

We also learn that Ballou preferred speaking extemporane-
ously in order to place himself closer to the affective impulses of his
audience and thus engage in interaffective creative engagement.
According to Ballou:

The advantages of extemporaneous speaking are doubtless
many. It enables the individual to place himself in closer contact with the feelings of his audience, giving him the power to
take advantage of any bright thought that unexpected
impulse might impart.[33]

Like Channing, Ballou held reason in high esteem. But Ballou used
reason to dismantle Christian doctrines that affronted human
affection as well as rational argument. Ballou writes:

The doctrine of man's native depravity, of original sin, of the
deserts of eternal misery, of the vicarious sufferings of Christ,
by which he endured in man's stead . . . also, the doctrine of
the Trinity, holding that Christ is equal to God. . . . All these

notions, as it appeared to me, were essential errors, con-
stituting a mass of confusion. I soon renounced all these
views. . . . All my brethren in the ministry, and all our friends,
stood on the old platform, and I found that I had to contend
with Universalists as well as with partialists. But I went to my
work in earnest, laboring with all my skill and with all my
limited talents, to convince my brethren in the ministry, and
all who heard me, that the doctrines of the Trinity, of depravity, of eternal penalty, etc., were neither the doctrines of the
Scriptures nor of reason.[34]

Thus we might speculate that Ballou's doctrine of human nature
describes the continuity of being he experienced in his own life-
enhancing caretaking environments. From this perspective, we
can imagine why Ballou's call for an embodied theology of salvation might have seemed life threatening to Channing. Ballou's
theology would have challenged the uneasy truce Channing had
sustained between his own disembodied mind and his broken-
hearted affections.

Using the perspective of Affect Theology, we see stages rather
than divisions. Each man seems to describe a different state of the
self's development and each man seems to have created a rational
theological vocabulary to explain and justify it. The respective
theological positions of Channing and Ballou refer to different
matrices of human development.

These developmental matrices do not mean we presume a
single psychological line of development for human beings. Such a
claim, as Arnold Goldberg observes, is anachronistic: "Efforts to
delineate stages, phases, and hierarchies [of human, psychological
development] now seem obsolete and unwarranted (Goldberg,
24). Developing psyches, Goldberg argues, use whatever is available. Thus, the very concept of a "development line has outlived its
usefulness."

Affect theorist and psychoanalyst Michael Franz Basch adds
nuance to the current discussion about human development by
focusing the discussion more precisely on "affective development"

(Basch, 144) and "developmental arrest" (Basch, 133) in patients who are "ashamed of affect and overcontrol their affective responses" (Basch, 132). Basch writes:

> This condition commonly stems from affective understimu-lation infancy and/or from a parent's intolerance for the baby's affective expression—an intolerance that results in *arrest in development,* which later interferes with the transition from affect to feeling (affect is experienced but cannot be talked about or recognized readily or effectively). Unable to deal competently with this transition, these patients defend themselves by withdrawing from affect or its stimulation. Consequently, their inner life is impoverished, and their relative ability to identify and express their affective reactions makes it difficult to relate to others in meaningful depth. Usually in good control of themselves, these are responsible, hardworking, productive people. However, there seems to be little joy or satisfaction in their lives; they are chronically bored and sad. They are slaves to duty and lost without it.... When the therapist can help these patients to overcome their shame or fear of affective responsiveness by helping them consciously to experience and then to articulate their affective reactions, the results are usually gratifying for both patient and therapist (Basch, 132; emphasis added).

Basch, unlike Goldberg, focuses on the patterning principles entailed in affective development. Basch's affirmation of the developmental process thus pertains to the neurochemical and neurobiological aspects of the human organism as related to psychological development. Basch thus affirms the developmental matrices of human organisms that not only give us the capacity to walk and talk, but also to smile and frown and to consciously reflect upon affective states and express them as conscious feelings.

Affect Theology, building on contemporary psychological studies of human affect, uses the term *developmental matrices* to acknowledge the different ways in which Channing and Ballou seemed to link their personal affections, theological conceptions, and social histories together. Channing sanctioned a theology that did battle against one's own affections. Ballou espoused a theology that aligned thoughts and affections. Both men thus engaged human affections. This engagement (and attempted disengagement) is the biological foundation of their respective theological claims. Their theologies describe their respective developmental matrices of the ongoing process of human engagement and disengagement with affect.

We might conclude that both Ballou and Channing endeavored to affirm the continuity of human experience in their own terms. We will never know if our hypotheses about the actual affective states and dispositions of Channing and Ballou are true.

Nevertheless, Channing's theology is consistent with what can happen to those who are forced to live in a nonnurturing, affectively cold environment. Ballou's theology, on the other hand, is congruent with the self-continuity of persons who have experienced sustained life-affirming affective engagements. Such persons, as embodied beings, affirm embodied theologies. Ballou, like Channing, was progressive and he was "heartily opposed to slavery"(Miller, 610). But unlike Channing, Ballou did not believe that the slavery issue should be an institutional concern of his denomination. He thus refused to sign the roll at the 1842 Universalist Anti-Slavery Convention, arguing, as Russell Miller notes, that "slavery was not a proper denominational question."

So who is the sinner here? Who is the saved? Clearly, the use of the terms *sin* and *salvation* outstrip their usefulness when we use them to compare and assess the character and worth of these two men. Instead, Affect Theology uses the terms to assess and judge the affective social environments of Channing and Ballou. This assessment helps us understand the differences between the espoused theological doctrines of human nature according to Channing and Ballou.

Affect Theology thus enables us to resolve the disparate theological doctrines of human nature bequeathed to us by Channing and Ballou. We look to their lives rather than to their ideas to resolve the conflict. We discover the ways in which their own lives might have shaped their distinct doctrines of human nature. Their doctrines are not in conflict, we conclude. Rather, their life experiences differed. Their lives illuminate their respective doctrines of human nature. Thus the legacy they bequeathed to us is not theologically conflicted but experientially descriptive of different states of human experience. All of our theologies describe the diversity of our life experiences.

Remember this diversity. Pay attention to the social contexts. Keep eyes focused on the people. Speak with compassionate understanding and our new words for life will include us all, ever anew.

Notes

[1] There are many persons without whom this project would have been impossible. I would especially like to thank my former research assistants the Rev. Dr. Paul Curtis Carroll, Jr., for his primary research on this project and Danielle Gerrior, for her further research and ongoing editing, commentary, and advice throughout several various developmental stages of this essay. I make special thanks to the Rev. Robert Hill for his detailed editorial suggestions and extraordinary attention to the overall structure and flow of this essay. My gratitude as well goes to the Rev. Tom Owen-Towle for his reading and reflections. I am deeply grateful to Constance Grant for her editorial skills and advice in working through the final draft of this essay. I thank the New York State Convention of Universalists for the opportunity to present an earlier version of this paper in October 2002 as the keynote address of their annual meeting. This present essay is an amended and expanded version of this keynote address with additional work from my essay, "Schleiermacher's Affect Theology," presented at the 2002 annual meeting of the American Academy of Religion. Special thanks to Walter Balk for critical reviews of this Schleiermacher essay and for his refinements of my translations of German passages included in the essay.

[2] Martin Luther, *Luther's Works* (Philadelphia: Muhlenberg Press, 1958), pp. 32, 112–113. Cited by Richard H. Popkin in *The History of Scepticism from Erasmus to Spinoza* (Berkeley: The University of California Press, 1979), p. 3.

3 Popkin, *History of Scepticism*, p. 3.

4 Martin Luther, "Against the Robbing and Murdering Hordes of Peasants: 1525", trans. by Charles M. Jacobs, revised by Robert C. Schultz, *Luther's Works*, Vol. 46, ed. Robert C. Schultz (Philadelphia: Fortress Press, 1967), 50. Heiko A. Oberman presents a fine review of the historiographical issues entailed in the dominant narratives of Luther's diatribes against Jews and peasants in *The Two Reformations: The Journey from the Last Days to the New World*, ed. Donald Weinstein (New Haven: Yale University Press, 2003).

5 John Calvin, *Calvin: Institutes of the Christian Religion*, John T. McNeill, ed., The Library of Christian Classics Vol. XX (Philadelphia: The Westminster Press, 1960), Book 3. Chapter 19. Paragraph 2. See Randall C. Zachman's *The Assurance of Faith: Conscience in the Theology of Martin Luther and John Calvin* (Minneapolis: Fortress Press, 1993) for a lucid analysis of the respective differences in the use of conscience by the two reformers. Calvin, of course, had Servetus burned at the stake in 1553 for daring to challenge Calvin's belief in the absolute divinity of Christ. So again, something about human nature was affirmed as the human foundation of religious faith, but *our* own contemporary liberal religious movement does not embrace Calvin's doctrinal legacy as the foundational insight of our faith. Daniel Walker Howe makes this point in *The Unitarian Conscience: Harvard Moral Philosophy, 1805–1861* (Middletown, Conn.: Wesleyan University Press, 1988), when characterizing the nineteenth-century classical period of Unitarianism of moral philosophy at Harvard as "a sustained reply to Calvin" (p. 49). Nevertheless, as Howe also pointedly notes, William Ellery Channing also celebrated the human conscience as man's "Likeness to God" and the "Divinity within us" (p. 53).

6 For a detailed discussion of Schleiermacher's use of this term, see my paper, "Schleiermacher's Affekt Theology," originally presented to the Schleiermacher Session on Practical Theology at the 2002 annual meeting of the American Academy of Religion. Also see Karl Bernecker, *Kritische Darstellung der Geschichte des Affektbegriffes (Von Descartes bis zur Gegenwart)*, Inaugural-Dissertation zur Erlangung der philosophischen Fakultaet der Koeniglichen Universitaet Greifswald (Berlin: Druck von Otto Godemann, 1915), for a more detailed discussion of the introduction of the term into the German language.

7 Donald L. Nathanson, *Shame and Pride: Affect, Sex, and the Birth of the Self* (New York: W. W. Norton & Company, 1992), pp. 54, 47–72. Also see

Michael Franz Basch, *Understanding Psychotherapy: The Science Behind the Art* (New York: Basic Books, 1988), pp. 65–99.

[8] Schleiermacher explains this approach of pious integrity and sympathy toward assaultive behavior in intricate detail in *On Freedom*, trans. Albert L. Blackwell (Lewiston, N.Y.: The Edwin Mellen Press, 1992). For a comparable approach from a Buddhist perspective, but one more accessibly explained, see Thich Nhat Hanh's *Anger: Wisdom for Cooling the Flames* (New York: Riverhead Books, Penguin Putnam, Inc., 2001).

[9] Lüdwig Feuerbach made this line of reasoning famous.

[10] See the contemporary classic text by developmental psychologist Daniel N. Stern, *The Interpersonal World of the Infant: A View from Psychoanalyst and Developmental Psychology* (New York: Basic Books, 2000), for a detailed delineation of the way in which the infant becomes coherent, congruent, and integrated to itself with its own personal history as an embodied being.

[11] Friedrich Schleiermacher, *Über die Religion. Reden an de Gebildeten unter ihren Verächtern* (1799), ed. Günter Meckenstock (Berlin: Walter de Gruyter, 2001), p. 90. English translation by Richard Crouter, *On Religion: Speeches to Its Cultured Despisers* (Cambridge: Cambridge University Press, 1988), p. 113.

[12] A fuller elaboration is found in my essay, "Schleiermacher's Affect Theology," presented in the Schleiermacher Session on Practical Theology at the 2002 annual meeting of the American Academy of Religion and my essay "Schleiermacher, Feminism, and Liberation Theology: A Key" in the *Cambridge Companion to Schleiermacher* (Cambridge: Cambridge University Press, in press).

[13] For a fine systematic summary of the rational foundation of Unitarian faith in the United States, see Gary Dorrien's *The Making of American Liberal Theology: Imagining Progressive Religion 1805–1900* (Louisville: Westminster John Knox Press, 2001).

[14] Raymond Hopkins, "A Functional Philosophy for the Liberal Church" (Boston: A Thesis submitted in partial fulfillment of the requirements for the Degree of Bachelor of Sacred Theology, Tufts College, 1949), vii–viii. Hopkins gives us the standard definition of *liberal* religion and the standard foundation for this form of religious practice. The term *liberal* is used,

Hopkins tells us, "to refer to those persons or churches within the Free Churches [i.e., progressive churches—rather than orthodox or conservative churches—that have congregational polity] who are not bound by established forms but rather seek a working faith by the free use of reason." The task of reason, Hopkins argues, is to "provide worship with new forms and new content that will meet the needs of men living in today's world and square with their highest intellectual insights." I argue in my paper, that these definitions make it impossible for us to solve the problem we seek to resolve: A sure, nondoctrinal foundation for liberal faith. For more discussion of the nature of Schleiermacher's "affective revolution," see Paul Adam Bernabeo's *With Blended Might: An Investigation into Friedrich Schleiermacher's Aesthetics and the Family Resemblance between Religion and Art* (New York: Dissertation for Colombia University, 1981). As Bernabeo notes, "The history of religious thought undergoes one of its major revolutions" with Schleiermacher's discussion of affect in Proposition 3.4 of *Christian Faith* (pp. 224–225).

[15] Paul Tillich called this self-critical necessity of Protestant theology the "Protestant Principle," which he explained as the need to undercut "the absolute claim of any doctrinal expression" because of the ambiguity entailed in any truth claim made by human beings. Tillich links this principle to the "prophetic freedom of self-criticism" derived from the biblical tradition. Liberal religionists are thus ongoing critics of their own creedal pronouncements. See Tillich's *Systematic Theology, Volume Three: Life and the Spirit History of the Kingdom of God* (Chicago: University of Chicago Press, 1963), pp. 176–177. Unitarian Universalist theologian James Luther Adams affirms Tillich's Protestant Principle when noting that the liberal Christianity Adams affirms and practices has a "principle that is creative but that also brings under judgment every actualization of Protestantism." See James Luther Adams's essay "The Liberal Christian Holds Up the Mirror," in *An Examined Faith: Social Context and Religious Commitment*, ed. George K. Beach (Boston: Beacon Press, 1991), p. 313. Adams, however, also pays pointed attention to the affective side of religious experience. (See footnote 32 for details.)

[16] James Luther Adams, "Human Nature," in *Voluntary Associations: Sociocultural Analyses and Theological Interpretation*, ed. J. Ronald Engel (Chicago: Exploration Press, 1986), p. 20.

[17] James Luther Adams, "The Voluntary Principle in the Forming of American Religion," in *Voluntary Associations*, p. 173.

[18] Adams, "Human Nature," pp. 26–17.

[19] Stern, *Interpersonal World of the Infant*, pp. xvii–xviii.

[20] See Antonio Damasio's *The Feeling of What Happens: Body and Emotion in the Making of Consciousness* (San Diego: Harcourt Inc., 1999), p. 287. Referenced in Stern, *Interpersonal World of the Infant*, p. xvii.

[21] Damasio, *Feeling of What Happens*, p. 286.

[22] Ibid.

[23] Stern, *Interpersonal World of the Infant*, p. 132.

[24] Allan N. Schore, *Affect Regulation and the Origin of the Self: The Neurobiology of Emotional Development* (Hillsales, N.J.: Lawrence Earlbaum Associates, Publishers, 1994), p. 7.

[25] Stern in fact refers to Demos's work when defining the matching structure of interaffectivity.

[26] See Stern's *Interpersonal World of the Infant* for an extensive analysis and discussion of the ways in which the self begins to form, cohere, and develop a personal sense of history and integrity.

[27] Heinz Kohut uses the image of a nuclear explosion to depict the power of the breakup of the "nuclear self," that is, a self linked to a formative other (self-object) as part of the self's own functioning identity. See *The Restoration of the Self* (Madison: International Universities Press, 1977).

[28] Judith Lewis Herman, *Trauma and Recovery: The Aftermath of Violence—from Domestic Abuse to Political Terror* (New York: Basic Books, 1992), p. 214.

[29] Ronald Story, "Harvard and the Boston Brahmins: A Study in Institutional and Class Development, 1800–1865," in *Journal of Social History* 8:3 (1975), p. 99.

[30] Maturin M. Ballou, *Biography of Rev. Hosea Ballou* (Boston: Abel Tompkins, 1852), p. 17.

[31] Ibid., p. 40.

[32] Ibid., p. 42.

[33] Ibid., p. 57.

[34] Ibid., pp. 70–71.

REFERENCES

Ballou, Hosea
1833 — "A Candid Examination of Dr. Channing's Discourse on the Evil of Sin." Boston: B. B. Mussey.

Basch, Michael Franz
1988 — *Understanding Psychotherapy: The Science Behind the Art.* New York: Basic Books.

Buber, Martin
1992 — *On Intersubjectivity and Cultural Creativity.* Ed. by S. N. Eisenstadt. Chicago: University of Chicago Press.

Calvin, John
1975 — *Calvin: Institutes of the Christian Religion.* Ed. by John T. McNeill. Philadelphia: Westminster Press.

Channing, William Ellery
1832 — "The Evil of Sin." *Discourses*, by William Ellery Channing. Boston: Charles Bowen.

1848 — *Memoir of William Ellery Channing.* Ed. by William Henry Channing. Boston: Wm. Crosby and H. P. Nichols.

Demos, Virginia
1984
"Empathy and Affect: Reflections on Infant Experience." In *Empathy II*. Ed. by Joseph Lichtenberg, Melvin Bornstein, and Donald Silver. Hillsdale, N.J.: Analytic Press.

Goldberg, Arnold
1999
Being of Two Minds: The Vertical Split in Psychoanalysis and Psychotherapy. Hillsdale, N.J.: Analytic Press.

Grund, Francis
1839
Aristocracy in America: From the Sketch-Book of a German Nobleman. London: R. Bentley.

Kant, Immanuel
1960
Religion Within the Limits of Reason Alone. Trans. Theodore M. Greene and Hoyt H. Hudson. New York: Harper & Row.

1993
Critique of Practical Religion. Trans. Lewis White Beck. Upper Saddle River, N.Y.: Prentice Hall.

Lifton, Robert Jay
1986
The Nazi Doctors: Medical Killing and the Psychology of Genocide. New York: Basic Books.

Luther, Martin
1963
Lectures on Galatians 1535, Chapters 1–4. Ed. by Jaroslav Pelikan. *Luther's Works Vol. 26*. St. Louis: Concordia Publishing House.

Mendelsohn, Jack
1971
Channing, the Reluctant Radical. Boston: Skinner House Books.

Miller, Russell E.
1979
The Larger Hope: The First Century of the Universalist Church in America, 1770–1870. Boston: Unitarian Universalist Association.

Morgan, John C.
1995
The Devotional Heart: Pietism and the Renewal of Unitarian Universalism. Boston: Skinner House Books.

Owen-Towle, Tom
1993
The Gospel of Universalism: Hope, Courage, and the Love of God. Boston: Skinner House Books.

Panksepp, Jaak
1998
Affective Neuroscience: The Foundations of Human and Animal Emotions. New York: Oxford University Press.

Schleiermacher, Friedrich
1830
Der christliche Glaube, nach den Grundsätzen der evangelischen Kirche im zusammenhange dargestellt 7 Aufl [aufgrund der 2 Aufl.]. Hg. v. Martin Redeker, 2 Bde. Berlin: Walter de Gruyter, 1960. English translation *The Christian Faith.* Trans. H. R. Mackintosh and J. S. Stewart. Edinburgh: T&T Clark, 1999.

1831–1832
"Ueber den Umfang des Begriffs der Kunst in Bezug auf die Theorie derselben (zwei Akademie-Abhandlungen mit einem Anhang) SW III/3." In *Friedrich Schleiermachers sämmtliche Werke.*

1981
On the Glaubenslehre. Trans. James Duke and Francis Fiorenza. Chico, Cal.: Scholars Press

Taylor, Mark C.
1984
Erring: A Postmodern A/theology. Chicago: University of Chicago Press.

Thandeka
1995
The Embodied Self: Friedrich Schleiermacher's Solution to Kant's Problem of the Empirical Self. Albany: State University of New York Press.

2002
"The Spiritual Life of Unitarian Universalists Lost and Found." In *A Global Conversation: Unitarian Universalism at the Dawn of the 21st Century.* Prague: International Council of Unitarians and Universalists.

Thurman, Howard
1971
The Search for Common Ground. New York: Harper and Row.

Wilbur, Earl Morse
1946
A History of Unitarianism: Socinianism and Its Antecedents. Cambridge: Harvard University Press.

Winnicott, D. W. *Playing and Reality*. London:
1971 Tavistock/Routledge.

1989 *D. W. Winnicott: Psycho-analytic Relations.*
Ed. by Clare Winnicott, Ray Shepherd, and
Madeleine Davis. Cambridge: Harvard
University Press.

1992 *Through Paediatrics to Psycho-analysis: Col-
lected Papers.* New York: Brunner/Mazel.

Wright, Conrad *Three Prophets of Religious Liberalism.*
1986 Boston: Unitarian Universalist Association.

THE LANGUAGE OF
REVERENCE DISCUSSION:

A Bibliography

Note: This list in progress, compiled by Dean Grodzins and Matthew Gatheringwater, provides the dates of publication or preachment, and, if the material was published on the Web, the date the site was accessed.

Arnink, Dale. *Religious Language: The Language of Reverence.* Unitarian Church of Los Alamos, N.M. (Aug. 3, 2003; viewed Apr. 28, 2004). http://www.uua.org/news/2003/vocabulary/arnink.html

Beaudreault, Don. *Reverence: Do We Need the Word?* Unitarian Universalist Church, Sarasota, Fla. (Nov. 2, 2003; viewed Mar. 24, 2004). http://uusara.lunarpages.com/minister/don134.htm

Bell, Chris. *A Language of Reverence.* First Parish, Cambridge, Mass. (July 20, 2003; viewed Mar. 24, 2004). http://www.firstparishcambridge.org/news/2003/06/01/SermonArc hives/A.Language.Of.Reverence-449710.shtml

Benner, Richard. *The Handle of Our Umbrella.* First Unitarian Universalist, Omaha, Nebr. (Sept. 14, 2003; viewed Mar. 24, 2004). http://www.firstuuomaha.org/files/sermons/030914_HandleOfOur Umbrella.html

Bertschausen, Roger. *Is There a Place in Unitarian Universalism for Traditional Religious Language?* Fox Valley Unitarian Universalist Fellowship, Appleton, Wisc. (Jan. 18, 2004; viewed Mar. 24, 2004).

http://www.uuwausau.org/Traditional%20Religious%20Language-Bertschausen.htm

Bietz, Gordon. *Reverence*. Georgia Cumberland Campmeeting, Collegedale, Tenn. (May 30, 2003; viewed Mar. 25, 2004). http://64.233.167.104/search?q=cache:E47PEmpInPMJ:president.southern.edu/sermons/reverence.rtf+Georgia+Cumberland+Campmeeting+SS&hl=en&ie=UTF-8

Brooks, Jennifer. *Reverence*. 2nd Congregational Meeting House Society, Unitarian Universalist, Nantucket, Mass. (Oct. 19, 2003; viewed Apr. 28, 2004). http://www.uua.org/news/2003/vocabulary/brooks.html

Budd, Daniel. A *Vocabulary of Reverence*. First Unitarian Church, Cleveland, Ohio (June 15, 2003; viewed Mar. 25, 2004). http://www.firstunitariancleveland.org/SERMONS/20030615.pdf

Buehrens, John A. *Hubris and Its Opposites*. First Parish (Unitarian Universalist), Needham, Mass. (Sept. 14, 2003; viewed Mar. 25, 2004). www.webcom.com/uuchurch/sermons/Hubris&ItsOpposites.pdf

Buice, Chris. *Winning the Peace (in the Middle East and the UUA)*. Tennessee Valley Unitarian Universalist Church, Knoxville, Tenn. (May 22, 2003; viewed April 28, 2004). http://www.uua.org/news/2003/vocabulary/buice.html

Capo, Tom. *Communal Principles*. Spindletop Unitarian Church, Beaumont, Tex. (June 15, 2003; viewed Mar. 25, 2003). http://www.spindletopuu.org/Folder.2003-06-14.2557/sermon_communal_principles.html/view

Carlsson-Bull, Jan. *Oh My God!* All Souls Church, New York, N.Y. (Nov. 30, 2003; viewed Mar. 24, 2004). http://www.allsoulsnyc.org/publications/sermons/jcbsermons/oh-my-god.html

Connolly, Peter. *The Language of Reverence*. First Unitarian Universalist Society, Middleboro, Mass. (Sept. 28, 2003; viewed Mar. 24, 2004). http://uumiddleboro.org/Previous%20Sermons/sermon%209-28-03.htm

Crane, Katie Lee. *Motherhood & Apple Pie.* First Parish of Sudbury, Mass. (May 11, 2003; viewed Apr. 28, 2004). http://www.uua.org/news/2003/vocabulary/crane.html

DeCoster, Alida M. *Are We Mystics?* Cedar Lane Unitarian Universalist Church, Bethesda, Md. (July 27, 2003; viewed Mar. 24, 2004). http://www.cedarlane.org/03serms/s030727.html

Duncan, Lucinda. *Learning the Language.* Follen Community Church, Lexington, Mass. (Dec. 14, 2003; viewed Mar. 24, 2004). http://www.follen.org/sermons/03.12.14_Learning_the_Language.txt

————. *Reverence Revisited.* Follen Community Church, Lexington, Mass. (Sept. 21, 2003; viewed Apr. 28, 2004). http://www.uua.org/news/2003/vocabulary/duncan.html.

Eckstrom, Kevin. [Religion News Service.] "Request for Reverent Talk Inflames Debate." *The Washington Post* (May 24, 2003): B9.

————. "UUs Asked to Reclaim 'the Holy'." *The Christian Century* (June 14, 2003): 13.

————. [Religion News Service.] "Unitarians Debate How to Talk About God." *The Los Angeles Times* (May 24, 2003): B32.

Finkelstein, Roberta. *And So It Begins.* Unitarian Universalists of Sterling, Va. (Mar. 21, 2003; viewed Mar. 25, 2004). http://www.uusterling.org/sermons/2003/sermon%202003-03-21.htm

Gehrmann, Axel H. A *Language of Reverence.* Unitarian Universalist Church, Urbana, Ill. (Sept. 14, 2003; viewed Mar. 24, 2004). http://www.uuc-urbana.org/OurChurch/Sermons/91403Language ofReverence.pdf http://www.uua.org/news/2003/vocabulary/ gehrmann.html

Gibbons, Kendyl. *The Language of Reverence.* First Unitarian Society, Minneapolis, Minn. (Oct. 19, 2003; viewed Mar. 24, 2004). http://www.unitarian.org/fus/sermons0304/101903.htm#101903.htm

Gomez, Enrique. *The Soul and the Language of Reverence.* Unitarian Universalist Congregation of Tuscaloosa, Ala. (July 20, 2003; viewed Mar. 25, 2004).

http://bama.ua.edu/~gomez002/soul.html
http://www.uua.org/news/2003/vocabulary/gomez.html

Higgins, Richard. "A Heated Debate Flares in Unitarian Universalism." *New York Times* (May 17, 2003): B6.

Hirshberg, Craig. *Reverence as the Language.* UU Ministers' Metro New York Panel Discussion, 2003 (viewed April 28, 2004). http://www.uua.org/news/2003/vocabulary/hirshberg.html

Hobart, James A. "Conversing in a Language of Reverence." Meadville Lombard Theological School Chapel Service, Chicago, Ill. (Nov. 9, 2003).

Hoddy, Linda. *The New Universalism.* Unitarian Universalist Congregation of Saratoga Springs, N.Y. (Aug. 3, 2004; viewed Mar. 25, 2004). http://www.saratoga-uu.org/Transcripts2.cfm?TN=serv0329

Howe, Sylvia L. *A Language of Awe.* First Parish Church (Unitarian Universalist), Beverly, Mass. (Oct. 19, 2003; viewed Mar. 24, 2004). http://www.firstparishbeverly.org/a_language_of_awe.pdf

Hurt, Kathy F. *The Zen of God.* Unitarian Universalist Fellowship of San Dieguito, Solana Beach, Calif. (June 15, 2003; viewed Mar. 25, 2004). http://www.uufsd.com/services/061503.html

Jones, Jim. "Unitarian Universalists May Add 'God' to beliefs." *Fort Worth Star-Telegram* (Jan. 13, 2003).

Kratochvil, Nana. *Reverence and Justice.* Harbor Unitarian Universalist Congregation, Muskegon, Mich. (Aug. 24, 2003; viewed Mar. 25, 2004). http://www.harboruu.org/sermons/s20030824.htm

Letters to the editor. *Unitarian Universalist World* 17:4 (July/August 2003).

Macdonald, G. J. [Religion News Service.] "Unitarian Universalists Converge for 200th Anniversary." *Contra Costa Times* (July 4, 2003; viewed Mar. 25, 2004). http://www.contracostatimes.com/mld/cctimes/news/6234796.htm

McTigue, Kathleen. *A Salute of the Soul.* Unitarian Society, New Haven, Conn. (Dec. 7, 2003; viewed Mar. 24, 2004). http://home.att.net/~usnh/20031207.html

Muir, Fredric J. *Watch Your Language*. Unitarian Universalist Church of Annapolis, Md. (Feb. 23, 2003; viewed April 28, 2004).
http://www.toad.net/~uuca/sermons/word.html
http://www.uua.org/news/2003/vocabulary/muir.html

Nelson, Clay. *UU Tolerance and Other Fairy Tales*. Unitarian Universalist Society, Sacramento, Calif. (May 25, 2003; viewed Mar. 24, 2004).
http://www.uuss.org/sermons/guestsermons/claynelson%20030525.htm

O'Neill, Patrick T. *Recovering a Language of Reverence*. First Unitarian Church, Wilmington, Del. (Oct. 5, 2003; viewed Mar. 24, 2004).
http://www.firstu.org/sermons/sermon_031005.htm

Paulson, Michael. "Words of 'Reverence' Roil a Church: In Boston, Unitarian Universalists Ponder Nature of Their Faith." *Boston Globe* (June 28, 2003): A1.

Payson, Aaron R. *Becoming a Beacon*. The Unitarian Universalist Church, Worcester, Mass. (Sept. 21, 2003; viewed Mar. 24, 2004).
http://64.233.167.104/search?q=cache:UG91vomFRJoJ:www.uuworcester.org/Beacon.pdf+%22Becoming+a+Beacon%22+Payson&hl=en&ie=UTF-8

Petersberger, Clare L. *A Language of Reverence*. Unitarian Universalist Church, Towson, Md. (Dec. 7, 2003; viewed Mar. 24, 2004).
http://www.towsonuuc.org/SermonDecember72003.html

Phifer, Kenneth. *A Theology of Sorts*. First Unitarian Universalist Church, Ann Arbor, Mich. (July 2003; viewed Mar. 25, 2004).
http://www.uuaa.org/sermons/a_theology_of_sorts.txt

"Reclaiming a Vocabulary of Reverence within Unitarian Universalism." Communications forum (viewed April 26, 2004).
http:www.uua.org/programs/discussion/language/index.html

Riegel, Kimi. *But I Like the Principles and Purposes*. Northwest Unitarian Universalist Church, Southfield, Mich. (Sept. 14, 2003; viewed Mar. 25, 2004).
http://www.mindspring.com/~northwestuu/SermonReverence.htm

Schuh, Shiela. *Living Words.* May Memorial Unitarian Universalist Society, Syracuse, N.Y. (March 30, 2003; viewed April 28, 2004). http://www.uua.org/news/2003/vocabulary/schuh.html

Sinkford, William. "In from the Margins." Religious Humanism 37 (2003): 44–52.

———. "Language of Reverence: A Response [to Rebecca Parker]." *Journal of Starr King School for the Ministry* [on-line] (Spring 2003).

———. "Share the Good News with a World that Badly Needs It." *Unitarian Univeralist World* 17:2 (March/April 2003): 9.

———. "A Statement from President William G. Sinkford." E-mail to the Unitarian Universalist Minister's Association Chat (January 15, 2003). http://www.sksm.edu/info/journal_images/sinkford.pdf.

Trumbore, Samuel A. *On Seeking a Language of Reverence.* First Unitarian Universalist Society, Albany, N.Y. (Sept. 21, 2003; viewed Mar. 24, 2003). http://www.trumbore.org/sam/sermons/sd93.htm

"Unitarians' Big Forum a Time for Questioning." *Los Angeles Times* (July 12, 2003): B23.

Walters, James. *Shedding the Shroud.* Unitarian Universalist Church of the Restoration, Philadelphia, Pa. (April 20, 2003; viewed April 28, 2004). http://www.uua.org/news/2003/vocabulary/walters.html

Weinstein, Victoria. *The Ungodly, Godly Principles.* First Parish Church, Norwell, Mass. (Mar. 9, 2003; viewed Mar. 25, 2004). http://www.gis.net/~fpnma/sermons/ungodly.html

Weissbard, Dave. *Did You Really Mean What I Thought I Heard You Say?* Unitarian Universalist Church, Rockford, Ill. (Jan. 26, 2003; viewed Mar. 25, 2004). http://www.uurockford.org/

Wells, Barbara. *You Matter to God: The Heart of Universalism.* Paint Branch UU Church, Adelphi, Md. (May 4, 2003; viewed Mar. 24, 2004). http://www.uua.org/news/2003/vocabulary/sermons.html

Wohle, Alison. *Not By Reason Alone.* Unitarian Universalist Church, Meadville, Pa. (Aug. 3, 2003; viewed Mar. 24, 2004).
http://www.uumeadville.org/Sermons/03aug3.html

Woulfe, Martin. *From the Minister.* Abraham Lincoln Unitarian Universalist Congregation, Springfield, Ill. (Sept. 2003; viewed Mar. 25, 2004).
http://www.aluuc.org/News2003Sep.htm

Zucker, Amy. *The Workings of the Heart.* Unitarian Universalist Church, Palo Alto, Calif. (Oct. 12, 2003; viewed Mar. 24, 2004).
http://www.uucpa.org/sermons/sermon031012.html

Contributors

Dean Grodzins is Assistant Professor of History at Meadville Lombard Theological School and editor of the Journal of Unitarian Universalist History. He is the author of *American Heretic: Theodore Parker and Transcendentalism*.

William G. Sinkford is the seventh President of the Unitarian Universalist Association. He has had a successful business career and a distinguished record of volunteer involvement with community action groups and not-for-profit housing developments.

David E. Bumbaugh is Minister Emeritus of the Unitarian Church in Summit, New Jersey, and Associate Professor of Ministry at Meadville Lombard Theological School in Chicago. He is the author of *The Education of God* and *Unitarian Universalism: A Narrative History*.

Laurel Hallman is the Senior Minister of the First Unitarian Church of Dallas. She is the author of *Living by Heart: A Guide to Devotional Practice* (workbook and video), and leads spirituality retreats.

Sharon Welch is Professor of Religious Studies, Women's Studies, and Mulitcultural Education at the University of Missouri-Columbia. She is the author of *Sweet Dreams in America: Making Ethics and Spirituality Work* and *A Feminist Ethic of Risk*.

Thandeka is Associate Professor of Theology and Culture at Meadville Lombard Theological School, President of the Center for Community Values, and the author of *The Embodied Self: Friedrich Schleiermacher's Solution to Kant's Problem of the Empirical Self* and *Learning to be White: Money, Race and God in America*.

Printed in the United States
115008LV00005B/182/A

9 780970 247971